CW01313342

True ~~Tails~~ Tales

Animal Adventures of an SPCA Inspector

Hugh Coghill

WESTBOW PRESS
A DIVISION OF THOMAS NELSON
& ZONDERVAN

Copyright © 2014 Hugh Coghill.

All rights reserved. No part of this book may be used or reproduced by any means, graphic, electronic, or mechanical, including photocopying, recording, taping or by any information storage retrieval system without the written permission of the publisher except in the case of brief quotations embodied in critical articles and reviews.

Author photo by Jennifer Funnell.

Circus inspection photos by Jo-Anne McArthur/We Animals.

WestBow Press books may be ordered through booksellers or by contacting:

WestBow Press
A Division of Thomas Nelson & Zondervan
1663 Liberty Drive
Bloomington, IN 47403
www.westbowpress.com
1 (866) 928-1240

Because of the dynamic nature of the Internet, any web addresses or links contained in this book may have changed since publication and may no longer be valid. The views expressed in this work are solely those of the author and do not necessarily reflect the views of the publisher, and the publisher hereby disclaims any responsibility for them.

Any people depicted in stock imagery provided by Thinkstock are models, and such images are being used for illustrative purposes only. Certain stock imagery © Thinkstock.

ISBN: 978-1-4908-2390-4 (sc)
ISBN: 978-1-4908-2392-8 (hc)
ISBN: 978-1-4908-2388-1 (e)

Library of Congress Control Number: 2014901438

Printed in the United States of America.

WestBow Press rev. date: 01/29/2014

Contents

Foreword ix
Preface xiii

1) Provoski 1
2) The Rabbit Lady 20
3) The Scarborough Budgie Lady 33
4) Strippers 38
5) The Lion Man of North York 48
6) Pomeranians! 65
7) Mr. Peebottle 76
8) Old Farmer's Syndrome 85
9) The Wolf Sanctuary—Part One 95
10) The Wolf Sanctuary—Part Two 102
11) Bull on a Rope 112

Afterword 119

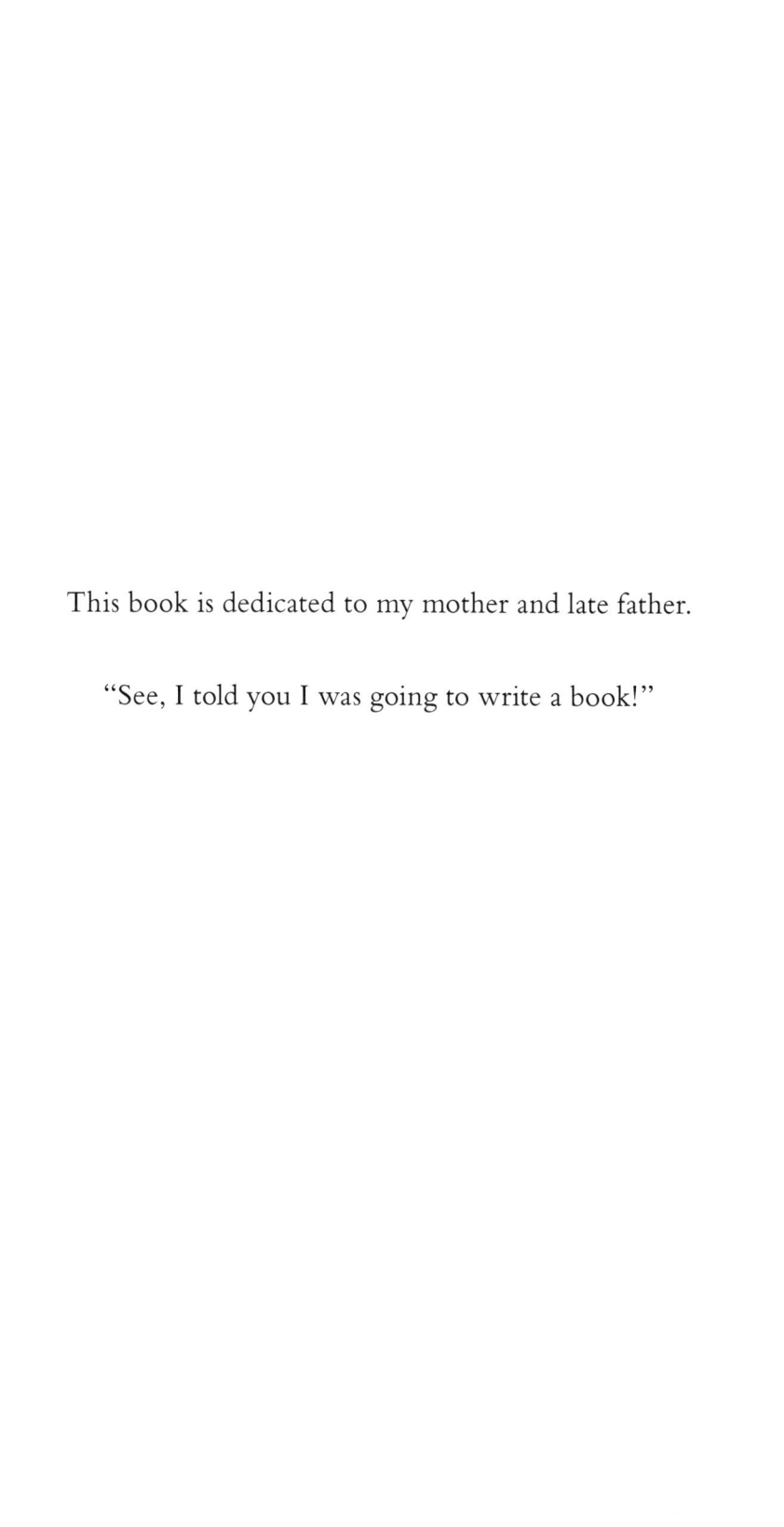

This book is dedicated to my mother and late father.

"See, I told you I was going to write a book!"

Foreword

While our species has excelled at many things, how we care for and protect the other species we share the planet with is not one of them. Every day, a staggering number of animals are killed by humans, the vast majority dying needlessly. Many others are injured, neglected and abused. And while our species' attitude toward other species is improving, we still have a long way to go regarding how we treat and respect nonhuman animals.

Hugh Coghill has worked with animals for much of his life. Together with his wife Christa, they provide a home for animals in need. Currently Hugh and Christa share their home with two dogs adopted from a rescue group and a cat who came from a humane society.

During the late 1980s and through to the mid-1990s, I worked with Hugh at the Ontario SPCA's head office. Hugh was the senior inspector at the time, while I was the publications coordinator and editor of the society's magazine *Animals' Voice*. I learned that the job of those who investigate cases of animal cruelty and neglect is a difficult one—at least for those who care about animals. Dealing with the numerous cases that are regularly reported is difficult enough, but those who endure such a job for any length of time will also likely have to deal with living with haunting memories from some of the worst cases.

One experience I had the opportunity of witnessing that has remained with me involved visiting two slaughterhouses in Toronto. Hugh provided me with this opportunity, for which I am grateful. While I am a vegan, I thought that it was important to learn what goes on inside a slaughterhouse. After all, our species kills billions of sentient beings annually for food, and a very small percentage of our species gets the chance to see how these intelligent animals are treated and killed in abattoirs.

While I wasn't looking forward to going inside these slaughterhouses, the opportunity of witnessing what goes on behind closed slaughterhouse doors was one I couldn't pass up. I hated seeing what went on in the abattoirs that day, but I learned a lot, which I shared with others when I wrote the article "Inside the Slaughterhouse," which was published in *The Globe and Mail* newspaper.

By reading Hugh's book, you will learn some of the things involved with animal cruelty investigations. In this collection, Hugh shares 10 of his cases, providing the reader with some insight into what cruelty investigators do.

N. Glenn Perrett

Glenn's latest book, *Hikes & Outings of South-Central Ontario,* was published by Lone Pine Publishing. Glenn is a frequent contributor to numerous magazines and newspapers, informing readers about issues surrounding animal rights, animal welfare, the environment, and sustainable life styles.

Preface

"You take this stick, go in the cage, go over to the den and give the tiger a good poke to make sure he's asleep." That was what Chief Inspector Hepworth said to me soon after he had shot a tranquilizer dart into each of the two tigers and a lion. All three animals had retreated to the safety of their den and were now out of our view. My previous zoo work experiences told me that poking sleeping tigers was a bad idea, but the loyal employee in me wanted to obey my boss.

Fortunately, all three animals were soundly sleeping. We set about the task of dragging their snoring, limp bodies out of the den and into their transport cages, which had been provided by the man from the safari park. Safari Mel said the male Siberian tiger was the biggest tiger he had ever seen. Having worked in several zoos and circuses, and having seen hundreds of captive tigers, I had to agree with him.

All three of the animals were now leaving the woefully inadequate, privately owned cage behind the house of the owner, Marvin Staunch of Sharon, Ontario.

The animals' new home was to be one of Ontario's accredited zoos.

This sets the tone of the 33-year career I had working in animal welfare, where I eventually became the chief inspector.

I spent the first 16 years of my life living in a part of the city that was occasionally referred to as "the slums of Scarborough."

Scarborough is a part of the city of Toronto now, but back then it was a borough, and we were proud to be distinctly separate from Toronto.

Although the housing was considered medium-density and the area was lower-middle class, my mother was proud of keeping a very clean and neat house. So when we had a pet dog, he lived chained to a doghouse in the back yard. That was more common then than it is now—thank goodness!

My parents were not "animal people," but I sure was— and I still am. My mother said "that personality trait skipped a generation," a fact borne out by my grandparents on both sides of the family, who were animal people by my estimation.

My grandmother on my mom's side of the family lived with us when I was a young boy. She just adored our dog and the budgie that we kept in a cage in the kitchen. Grandma spent hours teaching the bird to say "pretty bird." It was fun at first, but after hours, days, weeks and what seemed an eternity of the bird constantly saying "pretty bird," the whole family longed for some peace and quiet.

Grandma loved dogs and said to me one day, "Look at what you get when you spell 'dog' backwards." Grandma clearly thought that dogs deserved a lot of respect, as there was a distinct possibility of some sort of divine intervention that gave dogs their name. When one of my dogs died, Grandma comforted me by assuring me that all dogs go to heaven, and I would see Bowser again.

My grandfather on my dad's side of the family was a deeply religious man who read the Bible every day of his adult life. He raised budgies and canaries in his house in Toronto. He had built an impressive aviary, and the birds had indoor/outdoor access almost all year round.

Clearly my parents did not inherit those animal caring genes, but as Mom said, it skips a generation. I apparently got the gene.

At the end of our street, there was a forested area with a small creek running through called Warden Woods due to its proximity to Warden Avenue. I spent as much of my spare time there as I could. I was always turning over rocks and catching salamanders, snakes, frogs, minnows and crayfish in the creek. I gave them a good looking over and set them free.

When I was about seventeen years old, we moved to Stayner, a small town in central Ontario. My interests turned to my uncle Lloyd's farm and his herd of jersey cows. I have great memories of working on the farm, and of my cousin, Rick, and I raising and selling calves in order to make some money.

After high school, I only wanted to work with animals. I responded to an ad in the local newspaper for a zookeeper at a small zoo at Wasaga Beach. That zoo has since closed and all of the animals dispersed to other zoos, but I learned a lot about wild animals from a man who has been one of my mentors in life and is still a good friend, Tom Dunstan. Tom has an incredible way about him and seems to be able to communicate with animals at a level that always amazes me. This ability is often referred to as "horse sense," but I call it "animal sense." I credit Tom with instilling in me a constant desire to learn more about animals. Tom and I also both worked at the Toronto Zoo after the Wasaga Zoo closed, and although we both still support conservation and captive propagation, both of us have modified our philosophies over the years with respect to some species, but I digress.

I want to mention a few other people who have been instrumental in shaping my knowledge, feelings toward and philosophies regarding animals. Then I will get on to the rest of this book.

First, John Staples has to be one of the best farriers in the country—maybe the world—but I will admit that I'm biased. I worked as his apprentice and took up the hammer and anvil as a career for a while, but I was eventually drawn in other directions. Whenever John was perplexed with a horse or a particular situation, he would back up and say,

"Let's take a reading on this." John has incredible horse sense, and I believe that my own sense of reading what an animal is thinking—animal sense—was enhanced by his good example.

Next, Martin Cole taught me more about horses and how to be kind, patient and gentle with them than I could have learned from reading any number of books on the subject. When my thoroughbred stallion was of an age to start being ridden, it was Martin who agreed to ride the horse for me (I will admit that I tend to be slightly overweight and would have been a distinct disadvantage to the horse's ability). Martin was not only a more suitable weight, but he is an accomplished horseman with several British Horse Society degrees. He took my horse to a very respectable finish at the preliminary level of three-day-eventing in Canada.

One other close friend that I must mention is Paul Houston. Paul and I met nearly forty years ago when we were neighbours, both of us living on small farms near the village of Claremont. Paul had a small collection of pet snakes that he kept in his house. We both struggled with the "battle of the bulge" most of our lives, and I enjoyed working out with Paul in his well-equipped gym several times a week. Paul helped me to overcome my personal trepidation in handling large snakes, as you will read later.

I have had the great honour to work under the supervision of five Ontario Society for the Prevention of Cruelty to Animals (OSPCA) Chief Inspectors during my 30-plus years in animal welfare. Each of them taught me so very much, and I will always be grateful to all of them for their shared wisdom.

- Don Hepworth inspired me to put these thoughts into a book, as he wrote a similar book some years ago entitled *Gorilla in the Garage*. Some internet search engines will still turn up a copy if you want to read more SPCA/Humane Society-type stories. Don was in the British military and police before coming to Canada, and he was an accomplished horseman and marksman. Don was another person with keen animal sense who seemed quite adept at reading animals' minds.
- Hal Brooks is a retired RCMP superintendent whose career in animal welfare was painfully short (pun intended) due to a severe back ailment, but Hal was around long enough to put some proper police-type procedures in place at the OSPCA.
- Terry Looker another retired police officer, is from Zimbabwe (formerly Rhodesia). British by birth, Terry spent his working career in Africa and came to Canada too young to retire, luckily for the OSPCA. Terry not only had an incredible John Cleese sense of humour, but his calm, logical approach to the most outrageous issues and people was unparalleled. Terry was always staid and stoic, and he attributed those

traits to his being British. When I earned my turn to be chief inspector, I often found myself thinking, *How would Terry handle this situation?*

- Craig Daniell is a lawyer who brought phenomenal negotiation and communication skills to the position. Craig left Ontario and now heads the British Columbia SPCA. He has moved that organization to be one of, if not the, leaders in animal welfare programs in Canada.
- Mike Draper had a passion for animals all of his life. His time as chief inspector was much too brief. Some of the programs he started were finished by and credited to me, but they really were Mike's babies. Specifically, Mike started the OSPCA down a road of Personal Protective Equipment, and I was able to obtain government funding to enable us to provide all OSPCA cruelty officers with puncture-resistant vests, bite sticks (expandable batons) and animal repellant spray (pepper spray), along with intensive safety training delivered by a provincial police training officer. Mike also did a lot of work in creating revisions to the OSPCA Act. I was able to work with the government and provide my input, as well as Mike's ideas, to see those much-needed revisions put into place in 2009. Mike has gone on to work within the Ontario government still doing great work to help animals.

Prior to the 2009 revisions to the OSPCA Act, the Act had very little political attention since first being passed into law in 1919. I was working with that very old version of the Act, as well as the over one-hundred-year-old sections of the Criminal Code of Canada during my working career.

I spent an enormous amount of time on the telephone with and in person during the legislative process with Mike Zimmerman, who created the revised Act. Mike may be the only bureaucrat with such a strong sense of animal welfare. When anyone tries to criticize the revised Act, Mike is there to defend it. He continues to push for further revisions in the legislation that will improve animal welfare in Ontario.

My daughter Jennifer Funnell was always interested in the work that I do and welcomed any new animal that I brought home from work. Jennifer would find a creative name and help to provide the much-needed attention that those animals deserved. Jennifer kept me grounded and gave me a lot of focus in my life. Jennifer recognized that animal welfare consumed a lot of my time and attention. The time we spent together was always quality time, and I have great memories of us horseback riding together.

Finally, my wife, Christa Chadwick, not only knows more about dogs and cats and their behaviour than I could ever hope to know, but she is always my rock of support, critical sounding board and the love of my life.

Those people are real. They have all had, and some continue to have, an influence on who I am and what I do.

For the rest of this book, names (and some places) have been changed. The stories are true; they all happened, and I was either a key part of them or connected in some way.

I have tremendous respect for the field officers who dedicate their lives to working with animals in animal welfare, animal care and animal control. Recently an animal control officer in California was shot and killed on the job. My thoughts and prayers go out to his friends and family, but that incident demonstrates how difficult—and sometimes dangerous—the job can be.

When it comes to their animals, people often get extremely emotional. As emotion rises, logic and common sense diminish, as you will see in some of these stories.

After leaving my employment at the small zoo in central Ontario, I went to work at the Toronto Zoo. During my time there, I worked with many of the animals in the live collections. I still have contacts within the zoo world and enjoy visiting *good* zoos. Sadly, there are some pretty miserable zoos. I believe that we must all work to improve the conditions for all animals in any way we can.

I mentioned earlier that I tried my hand as a farrier after my apprenticeship with John Staples. Unfortunately, the hoof tends to grow slower during the winter months in our cold climate, and many horse owners pull the shoes off their horses for the winter. As my meager business slowed to a trickle, I was in search of a full-time job. I responded to a newspaper ad for an animal control officer.

I started work at a branch of the OSPCA as an animal control officer on the 17th day of the 7th month in 1977. I have often told people that with all those sevens in the start date, it must have been my good luck charm to give me longevity in the business.

Over the years, I have worked in the kennels and been a branch manager, cruelty officer (agent or inspector) and eventually the chief inspector. There is an old saying that goes: "The higher you go, the closer you are to the door." Like most of my chief inspector predecessors, eventually the end of my time with the OSPCA arrived. I continue to work for other SPCA and humane organizations and am currently enjoying some part-time teaching of Animal Ethics and Wildlife Management at a community college.

The stories that follow all happened during my time as an OSPCA inspector or as the chief inspector, supervising the more than100 cruelty officers across the province of Ontario.

Ontario is a huge province with around 13 million people spread across 1,076,395 square kilometers or 415,598 square miles—nearly twice the size of the state of Texas.

Animal welfare law enforcement is delivered by a network of branches of the OSPCA and independent Humane Societies affiliated to the provincial organization—all registered charities reliant on public donations.

The appointed officers have the authority of a police officer while enforcing animal-related laws, but they do not carry firearms. Training of those officers continues to grow and is in excess of six weeks, including some on-the-job mentoring as well as continued training.

Now that I have given you a brief history of my working life as well as a snapshot view of animal welfare in the province of Ontario, on to some of my adventures as an SPCA Inspector.

Provoski

Most people in rural communities keep a dog or two. Some keep a dog to protect sheep, cattle or other farm animals.

Few rural dogs know the luxurious life of their urban counterparts that cuddle in warm beds with their human companions who regard them as members of the family.

A dog on a farm or rural property serves a function—to sound an alert when a visitor or intruder enters the property. They also warn off wildlife invaders like skunks, coyotes, raccoons or possums.

The last thing the Evans family of Concession Road 11 thought they would ever see was a pack of nearly a dozen marauding domestic dogs come onto their property to attack and kill their German shepherd/collie mix as he stood firm, while chained by a 10-meter (30-foot) line attached to his doghouse.

It was about seven in the morning, and Albert (Bud) Evans was draining his coffee cup for the second time when he glanced out the kitchen window and saw the pack of dogs running at full speed up his lane. He knew instinctively that the dogs meant business and were up to no good. By the time he grabbed the cattle cane standing beside the back door of the kitchen and bolted out of his house, he could already hear the ear-piercing screams of his dog, Bounder, coming from the front yard.

As Bud rounded the south corner of the house, what he saw reminded him of the last time he took some hogs to the local abattoir for slaughter and glanced in on the kill floor. The pack of stray dogs was tinged with the crimson-red blood of Bounder. When they saw Bud coming, they hightailed it as fast as they had run up the lane just a few minutes earlier.

Bud knelt over his old pal and made eye contact as Bounder drew his last breath and exhaled one last time. His crumpled and torn body was such a contrast from the familiar sleek and shiny coat that Bud had known when he spent a half hour every day playing fetch with his beloved dog. Bud and Bounder had both enjoyed those few minutes of daily play and attention.

When I took the 9:00 a.m. call from Florence (Flo) Evans at my desk in the provincial headquarters of the SPCA, I could hear the grief in her voice and knew that she had a terrible incident to report. I could also hear Bud in the background, his voice raised and filled with rage. Flo struggled to tell me that their dog had been killed, right before their eyes, by a pack of stray dogs from "that place" down the road. I could hear Bud say, "Tell them his name—some kind of foreign-sounding name that ends with 'ski' or something like that."

I immediately said, "Oh, no. Not Mr. Provoski?"

Flo replied, "You know him?"

I explained that the SPCA had a history with Mr. P., as we referred to him. Flo said she wasn't surprised. She also told me that they had been calling animal control about the roaming packs of dogs. They had been told that the local municipal bylaws were very old and weak. There was nothing that could be done to help them.

The Evanses, like most farmers, were aware they could legally kill a dog that was attacking their livestock, but until the incident with Bounder, the roaming dogs had never been on their property—or so they believed.

I expressed my sympathy regarding the death of Bounder and thanked Mrs. Evans for reporting the incident. We had been wondering after our last dealings with him where Mr. P. had relocated. I assured her that I would be out the following day.

I had first met Mr. Edvard Provoski two years prior to the Evanses' encounter with his dogs. More correctly, I met Mr. P.'s dogs.

Before moving to a more rural area, Provoski had lived only a few kilometers from the farm home that had been shared by my wife, daughter, and me—along with our horses, dogs, goats and many other critters. Most of the animals had been adopted from the SPCA. Our livestock also included ducks, geese, pigeons, chickens, rabbits and guinea pigs, all lovingly named and tended to by my daughter Jennifer.

Early one Sunday morning, two good friends of mine, Dan and Don, appeared on my front porch with a plea for help from the SPCA. They had had enough of the incessant barking from the dogs on the Provoski property less than a half kilometer from their homes. In fact, the last straw was when they had both marched up to Mr. P. on his small, two-acre property to demand that he "shut those dogs up." Provoski was no fool. Seeing two farmers who were clearly irate, nearly twice his size and smelling a little like beer. Provoski stayed calm and quiet, but he then entered into a verbal jousting match that my two friends had no hope of winning. When one of them got right in his face and gave him a little push, Provoski smiled and said, "You just assaulted me." A couple of hours later, the regional police arrived, and both men faced common assault charges for their offenses.

I explained to Don and Dan that the SPCA didn't usually deal with noise complaints if it were not the animal control organization for the area. They told me that the local animal control officer had been called many times and that the matter was scheduled to be dealt with by the municipal council at the next meeting, two months hence. Like many other municipalities in rural or semirural areas, their animal bylaws were outdated.

I did agree to pay the Provoski residence a visit to ensure that the dogs were being given suitable and adequate food, water and care, as required by the Criminal Code of Canada. At that time, the provincial statute that dealt with animal welfare was woefully inadequate. There were serious negotiations being conducted by government officials to update the 90-year-old SPCA Act, but the hope of future revisions did little to help me at that time.

At nine the next morning, I called in to the office to advise my colleagues that I was starting my day by dealing with a local animal welfare issue. I informed the receptionist of my location in case I was not heard from in due course. I always think of my safety.

When I drove my SPCA truck up to the Provoski property, the gates were closed and secured with a chain and lock. Signs indicating that trespassing would not be tolerated were clearly posted. However, my shouts of hello toward the house, about thirty meters away, garnered a response, and a young man of about twenty, wearing black rubber boots, a red baseball cap and green coveralls was now marching down the paved driveway toward the gate.

I showed the young man my identity card and advised him that the SPCA had received a call about the dogs. I indicated that I was concerned for the welfare of the dogs and asked if he was the owner.

"Naw, my name's Tim," he said. "The owner is Edvard Provoski, and he ain't here."

After a few minutes of conversation with Tim, I learned some facts about the owner, Mr. Provoski. He was an architect of about sixty years of age, was originally from Poland, and had no kids or wife. He had lived alone since his mother had passed away, and he worked long hours in the city. The man was financially well-off, owned several rental houses in the city, and had hired Tim to look after his dogs while he was at work. When I asked if I could see the dogs, Tim was very welcoming but said he didn't have a key. He explained that I would have to climb over the gate. Having seen Tim's working attire and being familiar with similar places, I went to the back of my truck and put on my coveralls and rubber boots before climbing over the gate.

As we approached the house, the cacophony of dog barks and yelps was ear-piercing. The door to the attached doublegarage was wide open, and two farm gates had been tied with rope across the open garage. I could see that the door to the house was also open, so the dogs had free run into the house. The garage floor was wet, since Tim had just hosed it out, and the place was relatively clean. It was difficult to get an accurate head count, since my presence had caused quite a frenzy in the dogs. I looked at Tim and said, "I count about twenty-two or twenty-four." Tim replied firmly, "Twenty-six." My questions were all answered in turn, revealing that the dogs were all rescued from the pound. None had been spayed or neutered, at least two females were due to have puppies any day and they all seemed to be in good health. There was no shortage of food available; at least ten large bags of dog kibble were visible on a shelf in the garage. Six stainless steel buckets were tied to the fence, all full of fresh clean water.

From an animal welfare position, given the state of existing legislation, there was nothing I could do but recommend regular veterinary visits, vaccinations and a plea for spay/neuter surgery as we already had enough puppies in our shelters.

Tim firmly stated, "Oh, you don't need to worry about that. Mr. Provoski won't get rid of no dogs. See, here's the strange thing about him: he's a smart fella all right, lots of education, talks like a real big shot, but he has some weird ideas." Tim lowered his voice. The dogs seemed to be aware of the cloud of mystery and stopped barking for a few minutes.

"See, Mr. Provoski's mom died about a year ago, and he thinks she has been reincarnated into a dog, so he won't let any dog get killed in case it's his mother! He goes around to all the pounds and shelters and adopts all the dogs he can, especially the ugly ones that no one else wants to buy."

Tim had given the SPCA and me a lot of valuable information. As soon as I got back to the office, I alerted the director of operations so that he could send out a bulletin to all of our shelters and municipal pounds advising them to *not* adopt any dogs to our new friend.

I kept an eye on the Provoski property and noted that within two months of my initial visit, he had removed all of the dogs from the property and a commercial real estate sign adorned the gate.

My visit to the Evans farm was very productive. Flo and Bud agreed to give me a written statement indicating what had happened to their dog Bounder and that some of the dogs in the pack were thin, limping and seemed scruffy or mangy. Bud also advised in his statement that he followed the pack of dogs back to the farm on the other side of the road with the green, municipal number of 21928.

Armed with those documents, I attended at the local provincial court office and applied for an SPCA Warrant to Search for animals in distress. His Worship, Justice of the Peace Clarence Brown told me "off the record" that he was glad someone was finally going to deal with that situation. "My sister-in-law lives on the other side of that jerk, and those dogs have been crapping on her front lawn for months," said JP Brown.

I thanked the JP and now, armed with my warrant, called the SPCA head office and the provincial police for assistance.

Some people say they have to wait for hours for the police to respond to a call, but in my experience, when you say you are about to execute a warrant to search a property, the police are usually there pretty quick and usually in numbers not requested or seemingly required. The police have access to all sorts of computer-generated information and know if there are firearms registered at the property, if the owner has a criminal record or is otherwise known to police, etc. In this case, two cruisers arrived about the same time as three SPCA trucks and the local veterinarian who was specifically named on the warrant.

The gate at the end of the Provoski farm was chained and locked shut, just as it had been at the previous location, but we were able to simply lift it off its hinges and move it out of our way.

As the convoy of vehicles moved toward the house, several men emerged from the house. I had never met Mr. P. before, but I had seen him closing his gate when he owned the two-acre property near my home, so I immediately recognized him and approached him with a copy of my warrant. I explained that there had been a complaint about his dogs, specifically indicating hair loss, limping animals and sick or injured dogs. I introduced Dr. Bernard from a nearby veterinary clinic, and we proceeded to the kennel area. Provoski opted to stay in the parking area, chatting with the police and letting us get on with our job.

A makeshift kennel had been erected on this 100-acre farm. The sound of dogs barking indicated far more dogs than I had experienced in my visit to the previous Provoski property. As we entered the poorly lit kennel, the smell of feces and urine was overwhelming. Dr. Bernard had to step back outside to catch his breath and steel himself before attempting to re-enter.

Armed with flashlights, we examined and attempted to count the dogs. Some dogs were loose, having squeezed through broken wooden slats on kennel walls or sections of chain-link fence that had not been properly secured, allowing some of the larger dogs to push it out on the corners.

As we emerged from the kennel, one of my coworkers was approaching in full protective clothing of white disposable coveralls, rubber boots and gloves and a facemask. He advised me that the police were watching Mr. P., as he had been known to get violent. They could also hear the sound of more dogs coming from the house. I told him that our count at the kennel was 78 confined dogs and several running loose.

We returned to the parking area where the police were keeping a close watch on Mr. P.

I asked Mr. P. how many dogs he had. After a lengthy, cold stare directly into my eyes, he stated in a very matter of fact way, "I have about one hundred dogs."

I asked if there were any in the house, and he said just a couple of the small ones. I advised him that our warrant included the house, and we would be going in. This prompted a distinct change of posture in Mr. P. and apparently an increase in blood pressure, as his face and neck turned bright red.

When I asked if he wanted to come to the house to show us the dogs, he said no, but his hired man George would go with us. A wave of his hand and George was by our side walking to the house. Apparently, the employment of Tim, who I had met at the previous property, had come to an end, and George was the new employee.

When we entered the side door into the kitchen, as with the kennel, the stench in the summer heat was overwhelming. There was fresh and stale caked-on dog feces covering most of the linoleum-clad floor. As we went from room to room, we found bitches with litters of puppies and a total count of 36 dogs in the house.

Wandering loose around the house and kennel we counted at least 25 more dogs, bringing our total to 138. Once we were away from Mr. P., George was happy to tell us that Mr. P. had at least two other farms with dogs on them. George thought the grand total would easily top 200. He also said that Provoski didn't like vets or SPCA people because we kill dogs, and one of them might be his reincarnated mother.

Dr. Bernard had examined a total of 23 dogs that were in sufficient distress to require immediate removal to a veterinary facility in order that they may be given proper medical attention. I directed the other SPCA staff to begin collecting those dogs that our vet indicated should be removed. Then I issued Mr. Provoski with an SPCA Order to have the rest of the dogs examined by a vet and to clean the kennels and all housing to an acceptable standard. I advised him that failure to comply with the order within the stated timeframe might result in the removal of all the dogs.

When I returned one week later to check on the progress being made in his effort to comply with the order, Mr. P. was nowhere to be found. The gate was open, and the house was open and empty, although still covered with feces. At the kennel, my coworker Max and I found only six dogs in the kennels. For those six confined dogs, the feces was piling up, and the dogs had no clean area to lie down. Food and water dishes were all empty, and no food storage could be seen in or around the kennel. As we went about the task of catching the six remaining dogs, I received the second dog bite of my over 30 years in working with animals.

A very nervous Airedale terrier tried to get past me when I opened his kennel door. In my attempts to get a leash around his neck, he lunged at my face and planted a good bite on my forehead. This caused my glasses to slice down my nose, opening up a five-centimeter gash. I secured the kennel door and yelled for Max to come back inside the kennel, as I had been bitten.

I stood for a few minutes bent over the kennel, blood dripping from my face. When I stood to look at Max as he approached, he gasped and said, "Oh my God, we have to get you to a doctor." My response was that I was not going anywhere without that dog, since we had no idea of the vaccine history of these dogs. I was not about to start a course of rabies post-exposure shots if I didn't need to. If we had the dog, it could be kept in quarantine to ensure that it was rabies-free, and I could escape the incident with a few stitches and a tetanus shot.

After about a half hour, we were both soaked with sweat and smelling pretty nasty from being splashed with dog crap. All six dogs were in Max's truck, and I was headed to the local hospital.

I should say here that I am not a big fan of hospitals or of doctors in general. Having looked in the rearview mirror when I got to my truck, I knew that I looked pretty gruesome, with lines of dried blood on my face and strings of clotted blood hanging from my nose and forehead. When I entered the emergency room of the hospital, I anticipated a gasp and rush to render immediate care, only to stand at the counter while the nurse chatted with another nurse on my side of the counter about a wonderful recipe for muffins that they had both recently utilized.

The tissues I had brought from my truck were getting pretty soaked with blood, and I'm sure the air was rife with my distinct odor, but no one seemed to notice. I leaned in a little closer to allow my dripping blood to land on the counter. I finally interrupted the two ladies and apologized for bleeding on their lovely hospital, but as there were no other patients waiting to be seen, I wondered if I might get some attention.

Fortunately the emergency room doctor was less interested in muffin recipes. When she saw my condition, she started barking out orders to the two nurses. Before I knew it, I was on a gurney, in a treatment room, surrounded by a curtain and getting my face frozen by injections of some sort of drug. Seven stitches later and a lot cleaner looking, I emerged about two hours after having heard the greatest muffin recipe ever told. By today's standard, it is remarkable to: a) find an emergency room that is empty, and b) get medical care and be on my way within two hours. That was my lucky day and quite possibly a regular event in a small-town hospital.

The next day at the office, sutures showing and bruising coloring both of my eyes, I looked like I had just gone 10 rounds with Mike Tyson. My attention and concern, though, were for the nearly two hundred dogs that had disappeared from the Provoski farm.

Among the many branches of the SPCA, there are some very good investigators. It didn't take too long after I placed a few phone calls to half a dozen shelters for some good leads to come back to me.

I soon discovered that Mr. P. was well-known to at least four of our branches, as he had adopted more than one dog from each of them and expressed interest in several other dogs. Apparently the notice sent out from our Director of Operations had not been taken too seriously, at least at the four central branches.

Since more and more municipalities are becoming aware of animal hoarding issues, they have implemented numbers bylaws restricting each household to a specific number of dogs or cats—usually two or three. When an adopter adopts his limit, the shelter becomes concerned.

The latest intel came to me from Tim Monroe at one of our central branches that serves a large rural community. Tim was the only other employee beside me who had around thirty years' work experience in animal welfare. Tim had been a keen investigator, and although he was now more involved with shelter operations, he still kept his fingers on the pulse of the community. As luck would have it, Tim knew the property where Provoski indicated he was living and had taken his latest adopted dog to.

Tim advised me that the farm in question actually spanned over three different municipalities. Tim suspected this was an intentional ploy on the part of our infamous Mr. P.

With all of my documentation in hand, I attended the courthouse once again and was delighted to find that the presiding justice of the peace was Clarence Brown, the same JP who had signed my previous warrant.

After some discussion on the uniqueness of this situation, it was decided that I should have three separate warrants for the farm covering all three municipalities.

This time, in anticipation of conditions worse than that of the last farm, I arranged for a large number of SPCA staff and vehicles to meet at the local coffee shop and wait for my call.

Now, as I drove up the farm laneway followed by a police cruiser, Mr. Edvard Provoski was most surprised to see me. Instead of the usual pleasant greetings, I was met with a stream of swearing and cussing in several languages. It was Mr. P. who made the mistake of making physical contact by pushing me backwards, straight into a police officer who lost his hat in the struggle to maintain an upright position.

The police officer handcuffed Provoski and placed him in the back of the police cruiser. Provoski's cursing continued, along with the proclamation that this was an illegal search since his property was on three different municipalities. As I handed him three different search warrants, his cursing stopped, and he began a tirade of comparisons to the Gestapo, Nazis and references to his constitutional rights being violated.

As I entered the hastily built kennel next to an old barn, the stench was overwhelming. Now, instead of active, reasonably healthy looking dogs, I was faced with an uncountable amount of dogs that were thin, lethargic, vomiting and with matted coats. The sight of half-eaten carcasses of several dogs was all I needed to determine that my previously issued orders had not been complied with and that all of the dogs were in distress.

I called the staff who were happily chatting and eating donuts down the road, and within twenty minutes, a flurry of keen and determined SPCA personnel were gathering up dogs and loading them into trucks. I arranged for the dogs to be taken to several SPCA shelters that had previously indicated how many they could accommodate in the event of a large-scale removal. Many of the dogs required immediate veterinary care, and several spent the night on intravenous fluids at local vet clinics. All the dogs were given a full vet exam and treated as prescribed by the doctors. In total, 186 dogs were removed from this property. Together with the 23 removed the previous week, we now had 209 of Mr. Provoski's dogs in our care.

As is always the case, the owner is given the opportunity to surrender any or all of the animals on the promise that the SPCA would make every effort to find new homes for them. Provoski declined this offer and was served the necessary paperwork and advised of his rights to appeal to an independent tribunal before being driven away by the police.

The police laid several charges for obstruction and assault and released Mr. P.

After catching up on my paperwork, I drove back several days later to serve Mr. P. with his summonses for a number of cruelty to animals charges. Provoski was curt but polite when he accepted service of his summonses, but I'm sure the very large police officer standing behind me had a lot to do with that. One thing that struck me as very eerie and profound was the complete silence on the farm. The sounds of nearly 200 dogs were still ringing in my ears, but now this silence was deafening.

We never heard from Edvard Provoski or the "team of lawyers" that he had threatened us with. After the legal requirements were all met and the dogs had been nursed back to good health and body condition, all but three of the dogs were eventually spayed or neutered and adopted into new loving homes. Sadly, three of the dogs did not recover from their dehydrated condition.

I always attend court, even on the first appearance, for any charges that I have laid. The Edvard Provoski case was no exception.

I scanned the packed courtroom to catch a glimpse of Mr. P., but could not find him. When the court clerk called the case, a well-dressed gentleman stood and addressed the court, identifying himself as the lawyer of record in the Provoski matter. Council asked for the matter to be stood down for three weeks while he reviewed the disclosure (all evidence that the Crown will rely on at the time of trial). The three-week adjournment was granted, but only after the lawyer explained why his client was not present in court. Apparently Mr. Provoski was having some serious health issues and was currently in hospital. A note from his doctor was presented to the court and added to the file.

Subsequent court dates produced the same lawyer and the same medical explanations, along with doctor's notes and comments from the presiding justice that this had better not be a stalling tactic.

I don't usually read the death notices in the newspaper, but sometimes I read the notices posted by lawyers regarding claims against estates of deceased persons. One day, about six months after our most recent activity with Mr. P, I read a notice to all creditors in the estate of Mr. Edvard Provoski.

Apparently Provoski had no heirs, and his lawyer was not at liberty to tell me where his substantial wealth would go now that he was dead.

I often wonder about Edvard Provoski and his strong belief in reincarnation. When I reach down to pat our dog, Tilley, I only hope that she is not harboring the soul of Mr. P.

Incidentally, the dog that bit me served out his quarantine period disease-free, and I did not have to take the dreaded rabies post-exposure shots. This dog was deemed to be too aggressive to be put up for adoption by the animal control agency that did the quarantine, and he was humanely destroyed.

The Rabbit Lady

I am neither a psychiatrist nor a psychologist. I have had no formal training in the field of assessing the mental state of a person. The training period I received before becoming an SPCA cruelty investigator only touched on dealing with people who appear to have any sort of lapse in mental function.

I had to learn very quickly how to assess an individual and his or her mental state, particularly with regards to those who are aggressive or have a propensity to quickly become agitated. After all, we are meeting and dealing with people who are often in a fragile emotional state and quite often become difficult, to say the least, when it comes to the affairs of their animals.

One of my many continued training sessions attended over my lengthy career in the SPCA was with a police instructor who specialized in dealing with emotional or troubled people. I recall a specific axiom from that instructor that I fall back on frequently in life: "When emotion rises, logic falls." In other words, as people get more upset with me and/or the situation, their ability to think logically and comprehend a situation will diminish.

It is also important to recall that "as pitch and volume increase on the part of the other party, your pitch and volume should decrease"—another pearl of wisdom from that same instructor that helps to de-escalate a situation.

These lessons in life are very valuable, since SPCA officers in Ontario are not armed and are usually conducting cruelty investigation calls on their own. Two officers would be dispatched if there were foreknowledge of a difficult person. If the person were considered dangerous, the police would be asked to assist.

Marlys Wilton didn't fit into any of those categories, in fact, when I first met her; I thought she was a very intelligent individual.

We often get calls from the sheriff when a person has been evicted from their home and animals are involved, but this case was well beyond the usual few companion animals that people keep as pets.

Many people are familiar with the term *hoarder* since the broadcast of a popular television series that deals with that subject. There are lots of dog and cat hoarders, and I have also dealt with a few horse hoarders, but never one like this.

My coworker Max had arrived ahead of me at the suburban house and asked that I stop by the SPCA farm to pick up the truck and trailer. My cargo was to be rabbits. I assumed that the eviction involved a commercial rabbit breeding operation—until I read the address.

After hooking up the livestock trailer, a traditional four-horse trailer with an open concept interior, I was headed to the south end of Scarborough. This was not how I had planned my Friday. I always tried to avoid the city on Fridays if at all possible.

Scarborough is one of the municipalities that amalgamated in 1998 forming the Greater Toronto Area. Until that time, it had been a borough and then a city unto itself. Since I spent the first 16 years of my life as a citizen of Scarborough, I cringe a little when I hear the unflattering term of "Scarberia," and I don't like to use the shorter version, Scarboro.

When I parked the vehicle and headed to the house, Max emerged from the house and advised me that the place was full of animals, mostly rabbits.

Naturally, I expected to find rabbits in cages, either in or outside of the house, but to my surprise, the animals were all loose, running free throughout the house.

Clearly, rabbits had been living in the building for some years, as the accumulated, packed-firm feces covering the entire floor of the main part of the house was at least four inches (ten centimeters) thick. The heat and humidity from the effects of fermentation that occurs during natural composting had left a layer of moisture on all of the windows and walls. As we walked through the house, the floor had a distinct spring to it. Whatever flooring was under all the manure was obviously damp, as were the floor joists. I couldn't begin to calculate the added weight to the floor with all the manure, but I'm sure that the floor must have been near collapse.

Max and I secured the back ramp/door of the stock trailer and just used the small, man-door on the side to load the animals in.

The heat and humidity from the composting manure made the mild, early summer day nearly unbearable, so we were glad to be able to exit the house with as many plastic cat carriers, each loaded with as many rabbits as we could carry, every few minutes.

After about six hours of exhausting work, we were sure we had all the animals out of the house. Our final total: 88 rabbits, 1 domestic pekin duck, 1 grey, shorthaired cat and 1 beagle/terrier dog.

The representative from the sheriff's office had supervised, but not lifted one finger to help, the entire operation. To be fair, he found the whole matter quite disgusting and kept retching as though he were about to vomit at any moment. In my job, I have been downwind from many ghastly sights and odors, but one thing I cannot tolerate is vomit, so I was happy that the ashen-faced officer stayed out of our way.

When I asked the officer for the owner/tenant information, he advised me that Ms. Wilton, the tenant, had been there earlier but found the matter to be very upsetting and had left. The owner/landlord of the house had stayed away in order to avoid creating a "situation" with the tenant. An employee of the owner was due at any moment to put a hasp and lock on the door of the house, to ensure that no one would re-enter the building once the eviction was complete.

The SPCA Act requires that the official documents be sent to the animal owner at the last known address. In addition, an unofficial notice was posted by Max at the door of the house indicating that we had removed 88 rabbits, a dog, a duck and a cat. Should the owner wish to speak with the officer, my name and number were also on the notice, as Max was due to start his two-week vacation at the end of that day.

When we returned to the SPCA farm and shelter in Newmarket, the dog and cat were taken to the shelter and the duck went to the barn. We had four empty horse box stalls, so we decided that we would determine the sex of the rabbits and split them into two stalls each of males (bucks) and females (does) to avoid any procreation of our new charges.

It was nice to see the rabbits exploring their new surroundings in the deep, clean wheat straw that we had bedded the stalls in. Fortunately, these stalls have concrete floors, so "digging out" wasn't an issue, but digging into the bed of straw seemed to occupy much of their attention. Some fresh hay, rabbit pellets, several automatic waterers and a few carrots in each stall rounded out the day. I was happy to head home and have a shower.

Ms. Wilton, now homeless, had little choice but to sleep on a park bench in one of Scarborough's parks. She was able to use public washroom facilities. Early Sunday morning, she decided that she was going home.

The cheap hasp and lock on the door were easy to pry off, even for a woman of about sixty years. She had tended to her animals most of her life and was in good physical condition.

I discovered this information when I went to work on Monday morning.

After checking on the cat and dog in the shelter, I wandered over to the barn, where I met Sally, our extremely adept farmhand. Sally had a big grin on her face when she asked me how many rabbits we had removed.

I knew this one and proudly stated, "Eighty-eight."

"Nope," said Sally. "My bet is well over one hundred, but I don't want to disturb them yet."

With a frown on my face, I peered into the first stall to discover that in three corners of the stall, a fluffy rabbit-hair nest had been created. Suddenly I remembered how heavy some of the rabbits had felt when I picked them up last Friday. Between the two stalls of doe rabbits, we counted five maternity nests, but I agreed to leave them alone for the time being.

Sally was eager to share some of her vast knowledge of livestock with me and asked, "Do you know what it is called when a rabbit gives birth"?

"You mean, like a mare foaling or a cow calving?" I said.

"Yeah, or a goat kidding or a sheep lambing," she replied.

"No, I'm afraid I don't know that one."

"Well, it's called 'kindling,' just like firewood," she said.

"Great." With my knowledge of gestation periods, I figured we had about thirty more days of possible kindling to contend with.

Suitably impressed with my newfound knowledge, I walked across the parking lot and into the provincial office. After pouring myself a cup of coffee, I headed downstairs to the office that I shared with Max. Once settled, I had to look up *kindling* just to be sure that Sally wasn't pulling my leg. She was very knowledgeable but also had a wicked sense of humor and loved showing up the inspectors.

Before I could sort out my list of things to do this Monday morning, I received a phone call from a Toronto police officer working from one of the Scarborough detachments. Apparently Ms. Wilton, now commonly referred to as "the rabbit lady," had been arrested for trespass over the weekend. The officer advised me that Wilton was still in custody, and he wished to have a conversation with me in person.

I was eager to respond to his request, and not just to answer his questions. I was also keen to serve Ms. Marlys Wilton with her official SPCA documents in person. The quicker she was served with the documents, the quicker we could resolve the matter and either return the animals or place them up for adoption. As the animals were now increasing in number, this was going to become a problem for the SPCA—dealing with cost increases and space limitations. More important in my mind, it wasn't fair to all of the animals, dog and cat included, to be held at our facility when they could be adopted to new homes just as soon as the legal period had lapsed.

As I had other routine calls in the same area, I was soon headed down the highway to Scarborough with my official SPCA notices properly made out to Ms. Marlys Wilton at her last known address.

When I arrived at the police station, I asked the desk sergeant if Ms. Wilton was still in custody.

"Who?" was all he said. I started to describe the rabbit lady.

"Oh her!" he said. "She cost us five dinners last night!"

"I'm sorry?" I said, not knowing what he was talking about.

"Well, we just had five quarter-chicken dinners delivered from Swiss Chalet when one of our officers brings that old bunny broad in here. She stunk the whole place up so bad, we all threw our dinners in the garbage. The guy that brought her in refused to go back out until his cruiser could be cleaned."

The sergeant went on to tell me that Ms. Wilton had broken back into her house to see if all the animals were gone. She was in there when the landlord arrived with a builder and engineer to see if the house could be salvaged.

After the engineer advised that the house would have to be demolished, the owner became most irate and called the police to have Ms. Wilton charged with breaking and entering.

"Well, I haven't actually met Ms. Wilton, but I did see the house she was living in. It is rather important that I serve her with some documents," I said.

"I'm afraid yer outta luck, my friend. The judge sprung her loose about an hour ago," the sergeant said, "but you should be able to find her, cause she's wandering around her old neighborhood like a lost puppy." I suppose that was his attempt at some SPCA humour.

When Wilton's case had been called up for a bail hearing early Monday morning, the Crown prosecutor asked the justice to have Wilton remanded in custody for a psychiatric assessment. The justice now had a 60-year-old woman, well-dressed, soft-spoken, standing before him in a well-ventilated courtroom and clearly standing downwind from him, so he denied that condition and ordered her released, with a promise to appear at a future date to answer to the trespass charge.

I decided to take a chance and drive by the rabbit house. The doors and windows were now covered with plywood and bright-red "DANGER—UNSAFE TO ENTER" signs were conspicuously posted around the property. As I was leaving the area, I saw a lady walking along the sidewalk of the next street over from the rabbit house.

I took a chance that it might be her and drove up beside her. I got out of my car and asked, "Are you Ms. Wilton? Ms. Marlys Wilton?"

Now I was downwind from her and almost certain that I was speaking to the Scarborough rabbit lady known as Ms. Marlys Wilton.

She appeared clean, with what was likely very long, grey hair now tied back tight in a large bun at the back of her head. She wore a blue print, calf-length dress and what I call "grandma shoes."

Although her posture had been quite erect as she walked down the street, she now bent over at the waist, tilted her head to the side and closed one eye as she look at me and said in a soft voice, "I am Marlys Wilton. How can I help you?" Her icy blue eyes kept widening like saucers and then squinting into thin slits.

I took a half step back as I advised her that I was from the SPCA and had her animals in our custody. I handed her the two SPCA documents, which she took from me. Then she asked how all of her animals were doing.

I explained that we had set them up in separate stalls, and they were all doing well, as were the dog, the duck and the cat.

She shifted her weight, glanced around the street as if looking to see who was watching us and started to tell me her life story.

Her voice was very quiet, yet I didn't want to get much closer to her for several reasons, so I missed some of what she was saying. But I did pick up terms such as *gender specific segregation*, *coccidiosis* and *necropsy*.

Clearly she had been educated and had in-depth knowledge of rabbit anatomy. Apparently she had performed her own necropsies (the animal equivalent of a human autopsy) each time one of her rabbits died but was not able to find a laboratory that could confirm her diagnosis of coccidiosis (coccidia are a parasite of the intestinal tract).

While she was talking to me, she kept closing one eye, then the other, then both wide open, then squinting. From her bent-over position, she seemed like a fictional movie character.

Having served my papers and explained her options to surrender ownership of the animals or appeal the action of the SPCA to the Animal Care Review Board, or find a suitable location to have the animals back, I decided to get back on the road and complete my list of cruelty calls. I made sure she knew how to contact me if she decided to surrender any of the animals and said my good-byes.

Two days later, the daily reports from Sally indicated that our rabbit population was now in excess of 122. Sally was now asking how much longer this would go on, as she needed the stall space for other livestock.

I decided to call my friend the desk sergeant to see if he had heard anything further about the rabbit lady.

After he was sure whom he was speaking to, he said, "She's gone to the funny farm. I doubt you'll ever see her again."

Apparently, Ms. Wilton had broken into her house again and was rearrested. This time, the police officer called for the stainless steel paddy wagon to pick her up, and instead of taking her to the police station holding cells, they took her to the courthouse holding cells.

By the next morning, the pungent aroma of the rabbit lady, having not had the opportunity to bathe for a week or so, permeated the entire courthouse. When court was finally in session at ten a.m., despite the fact that nearly a quarter of the staff had gone home sick, the justice agreed that Ms. Marlys Wilton should be taken to an institution for a psychiatric assessment. Shortly thereafter, court was adjourned for the remainder of the day.

This was not good news for me. Now and for the foreseeable future, Ms. Wilton's affairs would be taken over by the office of the public guardian. This bureaucratic process meant it could take weeks or months to deal with the ownership of the animals. I was aware of this fact, having been faced with a similar case several years earlier.

Sally was going to be really annoyed with me!

Fortunately for the animals and me, but unfortunately for Ms. Wilton, when I finally made contact with the social worker who had been assigned to her case, I was told that Ms. Wilton would not be available for some time. The office of the public guardian immediately surrendered all of the animals to the SPCA.

Sally was delighted, but the shelter manager was annoyed when I advised her that she now had over one hundred and twenty rabbits to adopt to new homes. The dog and cat were scheduled for their surgery to be neutered. After some local media attention, all the animals were adopted into new homes.

I was in the neighborhood about a year later and dropped in on the police sergeant. He was able to tell me that Ms. Wilton had been committed to a mental health institution in the town of Whitby.

I drove past the old rabbit house and saw that no trace of the old building was left. A new two-story duplex was well under construction. The new tenants should be able to grow some pretty impressive flowers in that well-fertilized garden.

The Scarborough Budgie Lady

One busy Sunday afternoon at one of the larger Scarborough hospitals, a security officer on duty in the main lobby noticed a lady who seemed to be lost.

When he approached the well-dressed, well-groomed elderly lady of about seventy years, he asked if he could help her in any way.

She was very disoriented and confused, and she began to speak incoherent babble and nonsense to the officer.

He had seen similar behaviour before and knew exactly what to do. He asked the nice lady to come over to his desk with him while he made a phone call.

When the nurse on the seventh floor answered the phone, the security officer said, "We've got one of yours wandering around down here in the lobby."

The nurse assured the officer that all the patients with mental health issues were present and accounted for, but she would send an orderly down anyway.

After trying to get some information from the lady, the orderly felt sure that she was in some medical or mental condition that needed proper attention. A wheelchair was located, and the orderly escorted the lady to the seventh floor.

Over the course of the next few days, doctors and nurses were able to get her name and address through her constant ramblings of life stories, shopping lists, descriptions of numerous relatives and an occasional show tune or hymn sung with perfect pitch.

Several times during her lengthy stretches of conversation aimed at no one in particular, the patient became very concerned and spoke about her "Jimmy" who was at home all alone.

It took a couple of days, but the hospital staff were able to assure themselves that "Jimmy" was her pet budgie.

Since she had no purse or any form of identification with her, they had to keep asking her where she lived, where "Jimmy" lived, where home was, until they finally got an address.

I was dispatched to the hospital, where I met an orderly who would accompany me to the home of the patient now known as Jane Doe, since no real name had been confirmed.

When the orderly and I arrived at the address, we received no answer at the door and went to neighbours on both sides of the house. The neighbours were able to tell us that Mrs. Webster lived alone except for her budgie, Jimmy. Her husband had passed away just short of one year ago, but she seemed to be in relatively good spirits, tending her garden every day. They could hear her play her piano and sing hymns almost every day as well, but none of them had ever been in the house or actually spoken to her in person.

We decided to try the door after our search under the doormat, under the flowerpots and the usual key hiding places on ledges, etc., turned up empty. To our surprise, the side door was unlocked. We entered the house.

Calling out, "Hello, anybody home?" we went through the living room and dining room. We finally found Jimmy alive and well in his cage in the kitchen.

Aside from a scattering of hulls of budgie seed on the kitchen floor, the house was immaculate. Everything was in its place, the floors gleamed, counter tops were clean and no dust could be seen on the piano or any of the furniture. Much like her personal appearance, Mrs. Webster was a very neat and tidy homeowner.

The hospital orderly found a set of keys hanging by the side door, and we made sure all of the windows were closed and appliances were off, and we left one light on and secured the doors.

I transported the orderly back to the hospital and took the budgie to the shelter at the head office of the SPCA. The orderly and I had exchanged names and numbers and agreed to keep in touch. I would let him know how Jimmy was doing, and he would let me know when Mrs. Webster was released from hospital. In any event, the legal paperwork would still be mailed to the last known address, as is required under the SPCA Act.

One week later, I received a phone call from a Mrs. MacIntyre who lived in Hamilton. She informed me that she was Mrs. Webster's sister.

Once the hospital had Mrs. Webster's proper name, they were able to search and find her sister. Mrs. MacIntyre had been visiting her sister in the hospital ever since and had also picked up her mail at her house. My official notice had arrived, and Mrs. MacIntyre was now calling to deal with Jimmy.

I agreed to accept her signature via faxed transmission on an SPCA Surrender of Animal form and promised that we would find Jimmy a new home.

Mrs. MacIntyre told me that after her sister's husband passed away the previous year, Mrs. Webster had not been eating properly. It had been her responsibility to care for her husband of nearly fifty years, and she always served him nutritious, well-balanced meals. Since she only had herself to feed, she had not been eating well. The doctors soon discovered an imbalance in her diet had caused the disorientation and short-term memory loss.

Once the hospital supplemented her diet, she quickly regained most of her brain function, but she was going to sell her home in Scarborough and move to Hamilton to live with her sister.

Jimmy was a lovely, blue-coloured male budgie, but many of our shelters struggle to find homes for the smaller pets. Fortunately, one of our inspectors had space in her home (she had converted one bedroom to an aviary with about a dozen free-flying birds from the shelter) and gave Jimmy a good home.

Strippers

There is a segment of the entertainment industry that allows people to make money taking their clothes off in front of other people—strippers! I suppose that the old saying "if you've seen one, you've seen them all" could apply to this industry, though as time and youthful attractiveness pass by, some of these entertainers use props in an attempt to introduce some novel creativity into their acts.

Unfortunately, some of these people choose to use animals in their acts.

The first I encountered was a matter of accident, I suppose, when a young lady entertainer had purchased a St. Bernard puppy as a gift for her little brother. It was her plan to give the puppy to her brother one evening, but during that day, she kept the animal with her while she performed at one of the local bars in the town of Whitby. One of the patrons was incensed that she had an innocent little puppy on stage with her and called the OSPCA. All of the male officers volunteered to take on this investigation, but the manager assigned it to me, probably because I was the only married officer at the time.

After introducing myself to the manager of the bar, I met the young lady entertainer in her dressing room. I'm happy that the manager stayed with me. After hearing the story of the intended gift and a close examination of the animal, I determined that no harm had been done to the animal. The bar manager was not pleased that the young lady had attracted the attention of a law enforcement agency and sent her and her puppy home.

There was another lady that had an adult Siberian tiger that she used in her act, which toured around the province. I believe that photos appearing in the local newspapers showing her boyfriend taking the tiger for a walk are what prompted many municipalities to pass exotic animal bylaws preventing similar animals from entering their jurisdiction. An adult, somewhat overweight, likely 400-plus pound tiger is no match for the 200-pound man at the end of the leash, should the tiger decide to take off running.

The passage of exotic animal bylaws is possibly what caused "Ivana the Beast Master" to select a domestic pig as the animal of choice for her act. Ivana was performing at a bar very near to the provincial office of the OSPCA (at that time in the town of Thornhill), and the CEO of the day was most annoyed when he called me in to his office.

His instructions to me were to "shut this thing down," even though there was little chance of me doing much more than making her provide proper food, care, etc., for the animal in question. The CEO instructed me to take a veterinarian along and suggested Dr. McMaster would be a good vet. He had livestock experience and had recently been hired by the OSPCA to be the chief veterinarian for the organization.

Dr. Mac and I headed south on Yonge Street to the bar in question and approached the manager in his office. The manager advised us that "Ivana" was actually Lisa and directed us to the motel room occupied by Lisa, her boyfriend and her pet pig.

After formal introductions, Dr. Mac set about the task of giving the 25-pound piglet a thorough examination. Lisa and her boyfriend had set up a child's playpen in their motel room for the young pig. They had a good supply of commercial hog grower ration, a tip-proof water container, a tarp under the playpen to protect the carpet and a nice nest of shredded newspaper for the pig to sleep in.

Lisa told me that her father was a pig farmer. She borrowed a weaner pig from him and used the pig in her act, until it got too big to handle. She then took the partially raised pig back to her father and exchanged it for another, smaller piglet. Lisa had been raised on the farm and was well-versed in swine husbandry. She gave us a pretty good description of how she used the pig in her act, which made both the good doctor and me blush, but made Lisa laugh at our reaction.

When we returned to the office, Dr. Mac and I prepared a hastily typed report for the CEO so that he could respond to the local newspaper reporter who had been calling him all morning. I caught a glance of Dr. McMaster's report and the final sentence, which stated: "Other than what appears to be a permanent smile on the face of the pig, it seems to be in good physical health." Dr. Mac has a great sense of humour.

Early in November, the temperature starts to drop and occasionally goes below freezing. The leaves have all fallen off the deciduous trees by this time, the sky is grey most of the time (that sounds like a song by the Mamas and the Papas), and we are all getting ready for the onslaught of winter. It was on such a dull, cloudy, damp and cold day that we received a call from a man in the town of Stouffville. Guido (Joe) Parsons was born in Italy to an Italian mother and British father, hence the Anglo-Italian name. When he immigrated to Canada, he adopted the name of Joe in place of his Italian sounding first name, but he was not able to hide his strong Mediterranean accent, which got much stronger when his emotions were stirred.

I could barely understand him as he told me that he owned a house in Stouffville that he had rented out to a stripper. The young lady had left the house empty and owed Joe a lot of unpaid rent, but his reason for calling the SPCA was that the stripper had owned a snake that she used in her act. Joe was worried that it was still in the house.

About an hour after getting the full address, I was in the lovely town of Stouffville with my good friend and fellow inspector Max. A call like this would normally only require one officer, but it was a very slow time of year for cruelty calls, and Max wanted to get out of the office and away from the boring paperwork that comes with the job.

Max had agreed to come on the call with me without asking the nature of the call or the animal we were supposed to be looking for.

Joe Parsons met us in the driveway and immediately started shouting and waving his arms about as his face turned several shades of red. Joe stopped at the threshold of the house and said he could not enter as he was terrified of snakes, so Max and I went in on our own.

Most of the furnishings were gone, but there was a table with a large, glass aquarium on it. The tank was nicely decorated with dirt, moss, branches and a shed snakeskin, but no animals appeared to be inside it. The lid was pushed halfway off the top.

Since Joe had told us we were looking for a snake, I thought I had better get a bit of advice from an expert. I was pleased to discover that the telephone in the kitchen was still in working order. I called my good buddy Paul—the snake man!

Paul assured me that the snake was most likely a boa and would likely be quite tame, since the stripper was known to use the animal in her act. We learned that information from several of the neighbourhood kids, who had now gathered around the house to see what was happening. Paul asked me if the house was warm or cool, and I told him that the utilities had been cut off for about a week. It was as cool inside as it was outside. Paul told me that the snake would be looking for warmth and that I should be looking up, since heat rises. He also told me that the animal would be very docile in its cooled state. I thanked Paul for his help, and as I hung up the phone, my gaze turned to the ceiling of the kitchen.

I pointed out to Max that one of the tiles on the drop ceiling was moved. I got him to help me get onto the counter so I could lift the tile and have a look around.

Bingo—there it was, all coiled up in a ball trying to conserve as much body heat as possible. I kept eye contact with the animal, but verbally relayed my findings to Max as I slowly reached out and took a good hold of the snake by the head. As I drew the animal closer to me, I figured its total body length to be around six feet. As I brought my head and shoulders back down from the ceiling, with the snake now dangling full length to below the top of the counter I was standing on, I saw the back of Max heading out the door of the house and heard him proclaim, "You're on your own." I had no idea that Max was terrified of snakes.

At least Max was considerate enough to get one of the local kids to bring a plastic dog crate into the house for me to deposit the snake in.

We posted the usual legal notice on the door of the house, and as we were about to get into our truck, Joe emerged from his car with a bottle of homemade wine for us. He was eternally grateful that we had extricated the dreadful animal from his house. Now he could re-rent the dwelling out to someone else. We declined the bottle of wine with much thanks anyway and advised him to include a no-pets clause in future rental agreements.

Max and I delivered the snake to our shelter staff, and they set the animal up in a nice warm tank in one of the offices at the shelter.

The staff had a connection with one of the local pet suppliers who specialized in feeder mice and rats that had been humanely killed, frozen and sold to snake owners for their pets.

Max and I sent out the usual notices to the former owner at the last known address, but we knew we would never hear from her again. The shelter staff would eventually have to find a new home for the snake.

Three days later, one of the kennel staff called my office and advised me that the snake had eaten really well. They wanted to change the bedding in the tank; however, every time they lifted the lid of the tank, the snake became very aggressive and they had to slam the lid back down. I offered to come over to the shelter and help, but as I put the phone down, I felt a chill go down my back. Max was not in the office, and I knew he wouldn't be much help with his fear of snakes, so I went on my own.

After careful examination of the situation, I instructed the kennel attendant to gather everything she needed to clean the tank, to close the door to the office and to get ready to do this as quickly as possible. When we lifted the lid from the tank, the snake suddenly became very active and was about to breach the top of the tank when I quickly grabbed it just behind its head. With its mouth wide open and me lifting it up out of the tank, it quickly began wrapping itself around my arms. I told the kennel girl to move quickly to clean the cage, which she did. As I returned the snake to the tank, it made a final, unsuccessful lunge at my hands.

We are fortunate to have several good zoos that are accredited by the Canadian Association of Zoos and Aquariums in our province—and one in particular that specializes in reptiles. When I called to ask if they would take the animal, which we now knew to be a six-foot-long boa constrictor, they said we should just adopt him out. Boas are very common pets, and many municipalities still allowed them within their boundaries. After I explained how aggressive the animal had become, they changed their mind and agreed to take the animal into their collection—*whew!* One less snake out there in the pet world for us to deal with.

The Author during a routine inspection of circus animals

Circus elephant inspection

Circus elephant inspection

The Lion Man of North York

He was a fairly small man, Paul Mankle, about five feet, four inches (163 cm) tall and maybe 140 pounds (63 kg) soaking wet, as they say. He was somewhat scruffy in appearance, having tried, with very poor results, to grow a beard. He thought the beard would make him look older, more mature and more like a successful businessman. He was wrong.

An adult, male cougar, also known as a puma or mountain lion, on the other hand, can weigh as much as or slightly over 200 pounds (91 kg).

Mankle always dreamed of being an animal trainer who provided animals for the movie industry. With Canada in general and Toronto in particular being seen as "Hollywood North" for many years, he was sure he could make his fortune in the industry.

He started small with his best friend, a small, black, domestic cat named Puss. Mankle had taught the cat to go to his mark on a stage, or any point on the floor that had been designated as the mark, like any good actor knows to do. He also taught Puss a number of cute tricks like sitting on his haunches, standing up high on his two back legs, laying down, rolling over, etc. But the act that got a bit of attention was when Mankle took Puss on his motorcycle for a ride and one of the main Toronto newspapers snapped a photo and ran it in the paper. Mankle had a proper helmet and goggles made for Puss and always kept the cat on a leash as he rode around the city on his 200-cc Honda motorcycle that belched out blue smoke and sputtered like it was on its final journey.

Together, in their matching motorcycle helmets and goggles, they were an odd sight to see and made for good newspaper fodder on a slow news day, Puss riding with his forepaws over Mankle's shoulder, carefully watching the road ahead.

When the newspaper reporter stopped them to get some details and permission to print their photo and the story in the newspaper, Mankle was sure this would be his big break into the movie industry. Surely some important director or producer would see the story, and he would have all kinds of movie work lined up in no time.

Work was something that had eluded the 30-year-old Mankle. In fact, his parents had very recently encouraged him to move out of the family home, in part because they were hopeful that it would force him to seek realistic employment, but also because of their only son's recent acquisition, a young adult male cougar.

Mankle had seen the ad in a newspaper and quickly responded: "For sale, young, male, tame, western Canadian cougar, intact, not declawed. All shots up to date, moving to the U.S., must sell beloved pet."

It sounded like the usual "dog or cat for sale" ad, but this cat weighed a hefty 185 pounds (84 kg) and was still growing.

The word "tame" jumped off the page and straight into Mankle's brain, where it quickly conjured up images of big-time movie contracts, lots of money and fame. He was going to show everyone that he could become a big-time successful animal trainer.

Scraping together the $1,500 dollars was going to be tough, but he hadn't survived for the nearly 15 years since he dropped out of high school without learning a thing or two. Besides, his parents were loaded in his opinion, and he could always manipulate them to help him fulfill his dreams.

Mankle couldn't resist the opportunity to mention his *big* cat, Zuma, a western Canadian mountain lion, to the reporter. Mankle the wannabe showman always referred to Zuma as a *big* cat and as a western Canadian mountain lion. It sounded so much more impressive than "a cougar."

Poor Mr. Mankle must have been disappointed when the photo and article ran on page six the next day. He had been sure it would be front-page news. He must have also been sorry to see Zuma referred to as a cougar and simply mentioned as his "other pet." Still, it was free publicity, and surely the offers would be forthcoming for movie work.

As time passed and Zuma grew to just about 200 pounds (91 kg), he was still young at heart and did substantial damage to Mankle's parents' house. Their once-prized living room sofa had been used as a scratching post so many times that they were past hoping to be able to repair it.

Mankle knew that the cat needed more exercise, and due to the constant complaints from his parents, he started taking Zuma on walks around his North York neighbourhood. North York is now a part of the Greater Toronto Area, but at that time, it was a city unto itself.

Unlike Puss, who weighed about 8 pounds (3.6 kg) and was manageable on a light string leash, Mankle used a heavy chain suitable for towing a car when he walked Zuma.

Mankle had been seen with his trouser legs torn and blood visible on his legs from the constant playing and practice attacks from his new pal Zuma, but he continued to take the cat on ever-longer walks around the streets with the hope of being discovered still burning in his mind.

Often pet cougars are overfed and under-exercised, becoming quite overweight in captivity. When Zuma was approaching 18 months and 210 pounds (95 kg), Mankle felt he had to up the ante a little and get more free publicity so that he could be discovered with his *big* cat.

Before the Greater Toronto Area amalgamation, there were a number of cities and boroughs, each with their own identity, not the least of which was the city of North York and its much-loved mayor Mel Lastman. Like most cities, the major newspapers usually had one or more reporters at or nearby city hall to get firsthand information and get the scoop on the competition. Mr. Lastman was always willing to speak with reporters, or so it seemed, and he was often quoted in the newspaper.

All of this seemed like the golden opportunity for Paul Mankle to get that much-deserved free publicity and his shot at fame, so off to city hall he went with his *big* cat, Zuma, and 15 feet (4.5 m) of tow chain.

It started off pretty good. A couple of attractive ladies on their lunch break from city hall came over to pat the beautiful animal and ask questions of the always affable and willing Mankle. Mankle had perched himself on the back of a park bench in the shade just outside city hall, with Zuma sitting tall and proud, surveying his newly discovered kingdom.

This was obviously another one of those slow news days. When the two ladies returned to work, they mentioned to the local TV news crew as they passed them in the hall that there was a cougar outside in front of city hall. That was a story waiting to happen in the opinion of the TV crew, so out the doors they flew—reporter, cameraman, sound man, and all of their related equipment. It was Mankle's first look at a real TV crew, and they were heading for him.

It was also Zuma's first time seeing such a group of people and equipment rushing toward him. He decided that they surely meant him harm and that he would leave city hall much more quickly than he had arrived. When Zuma reached the end of his chain, it snapped taught. Mankle was now face down, sliding across the concrete courtyard, hanging onto the chain for dear life. This is what happens when a 200-pound (91-kg) animal runs away with his 140-pound (63-kg) owner, wet or dry, now scraped, torn and slightly bloodied from the experience.

TV news cameramen are not usually "animal wise," but they are always quick to get the shot. This was part of the footage that was shown on the six o'clock news that evening. After being dragged about 200 yards (nearly 183 m), Zuma slowed down enough for Mankle to gain the upper hand in the situation and hook one foot on a small tree that had been planted in the courtyard in memory of some great North York citizen—a lucky break for Mankle.

Once settled, Mankle and Zuma strolled back to the camera crew. Mankle calmly gave his story to the waiting reporter. This was also shown on the evening news, and despite the trickle of blood running down Mankle's nose, his wildly mussed hair and his sparse beard, he spoke calmly and seemed nearly rational.

The next day, Mankle finally made it to the front page, but this time the headline quote was credited to Mayor Lastman. "The only cougar I want in North York is made by Ford and has four wheels."

That night, city council sat and debated into the wee hours of the next morning and finally passed one of the first and best municipal exotic animal bylaws in the province.

Mankle had to move or get rid of Zuma. Secretly, this must have given his parents cause for celebration, but as dutiful parents, they showed their sorrow to their only son and helped him pack his belongings.

Mankle had a friend just across the border in the next municipality, where they didn't have an exotic animal bylaw. His friend had always liked Zuma and had told Mankle that they could visit as often as they wanted. So off to the city of Vaughan—"The City above Toronto," as their advertisements proclaimed—went Mankle and Zuma in his beat-up old Chevy van.

By now, the calls to the head office of the SPCA numbered in the hundreds. "How could we allow someone to keep such a dangerous animal in the city?" "What was the SPCA going to do about this poor animal that should be set free?" These were the sentiments being expressed to our receptionist, Maud, who kept her composure and tried to explain to each caller that the SPCA does not create laws.

It was not an offense to keep such an animal in captivity, as long as it was receiving adequate food, water and care, according to the laws at that time.

The call that made its way to my extension was from a soft-spoken man named Brad. Brad was a good friend of Paul Mankle's and had been to visit him at Jeff Richardson's house—their mutual friend who lived in Vaughan. He wanted to tell me that Zuma was being kept in the basement on a chain that was no more than four feet (122 cm) long. I arranged to meet Brad and take his written, signed statement regarding the poor living conditions in the dark, wet basement. This statement and copies of the newspaper articles formed the basis for my SPCA Warrant to Search the premises of Mr. J. Richardson to look for animals in distress.

Signed search warrant in hand, I attended the Richardson residence with a member of the local police force and met Paul Mankle for the first time. All through our conversation, Mankle kept looking over my shoulder. I asked what he was looking for, and he replied, "Where's the media? Don't you guys always have the media following you?" I explained that it was not our practice to call the media, but they often scanned police-band radios. When they heard news of the SPCA, a warrant to search and animals, they would pursue that lead for a story. Clearly, they had better things to report on this day.

When Mankle lead us down the old wooden stairs to the dimly lit basement with its wet floors, it took a few seconds for our eyes to adjust and focus on Zuma, who was pacing back and forth on a wet concrete floor at the end of a four-foot chain.

As I began my usual course of questions to the animal owner in such cases—how old was the animal, what was his name, how often was he fed, what was he fed, where was his water and how long is he kept tied on the short line—the police officer began a long stream of verbal abuse at Mankle and poor Jeff Richardson, who owned the house and thought he was doing his friend a favour. At one point, Zuma rose and moved to the end of his chain, prompting the police officer to remove his gun and point it at the animal. We all urged caution and calm as we encouraged the police officer to come with us back up stairs.

His firearm now back in its holster, the police officer turned to me and asked, "Is it legal for him to have a pet cougar?"

I explained to the officer and to Mankle and Richardson that it is a municipal function to establish animal care and control bylaws, and that no exotic animal restrictions existed at this time in this municipality. I also explained that it was my duty to try to relieve animals from distress under the authority of the provincial SPCA Act. Mankle would be receiving an Order to take swift, specific action.

Mankle was to lengthen the chain to at least 10 feet (3 m), provide a dry, clean area for the cat to rest on, improve ventilation and lighting and provide and a constant source of potable water. This was to be done within 24 hours. Further, he had two weeks to provide a proper cage of suitable dimensions for the animal. We left less than an hour after we had arrived, with Mankle still looking down the street for his much-coveted media, which never arrived.

The following day, Mankle called me to enquire what a proper cage of suitable dimensions meant. I said that since he didn't know. I would get some advice from the experts and get back to him.

Before coming to work for the SPCA, my work life was all animal-related, and I spent several years as a zookeeper at the Toronto Zoo and the former Upper Canada Zoological Society at Wasaga Beach. This certainly didn't make me an expert, but it allowed me to maintain contacts in the zoo world. My next call was to the Canadian Association of Zoos and Aquariums (CAZA).

I was advised that CAZA was in the process of creating minimum standards but was not in a position to provide me with the details I needed at that time; however, the American Association of Zoos and Aquariums (AAZA) did have such written minimum standards.

My call to Wheeling, West Virginia, the headquarters of the AAZA (now called the AZA), was very fruitful. A fax with the minimum standards for medium-sized wild cats, such as cougars, leopards, etc., would be on its way to me forthwith, as would a computer disk with all of the minimum standards of care for all captive wild mammals for our future reference.

It turns out that the minimum size of a cougar cage for a single animal is very close to that of a single-car garage.

I called Mankle back and advised him that the garage on Richardson's property could easily be adapted to accommodate Zuma. Mankle was relatively pleasant and assured me that that would be done within the allotted timeframe.

By the time the date of compliance for the SPCA Order had arrived, I had received three calls from various media asking if they could attend when I went back to Mankle's property. Mankle had called the media, always looking for the free publicity, and told the media that the SPCA was going to seize his animal from his house, despite the fact that he dearly loved and cared for his western Canadian mountain lion, which was in excellent physical and mental condition. This was clearly a violation of his constitutional rights, in his opinion.

In my unmarked SPCA vehicle on the day of compliance, I took a drive down the intersecting street from Richardson's house. There must have been a dozen media vehicles with satellite dishes on them lining both sides of the street. I quietly drove back to the office, advised Maud that I could not be reached if any calls came in, and left the office for the day.

The following day, when I drove up Richardson's street with Dr. Clair Royle, an SPCA veterinarian, there was no sign of any media. It was 11:00 a.m., and the clear, sunny day was promising to be a typical hot August day. The same police officer who had accompanied me on the warrant was able to attend again. We hoped to find Zuma in a lovely new cage in the renovated garage beside the house.

After about 15 minutes of banging on the door, a sleepy, slightly inebriated Mankle answered the door. "We're here to see Zuma and the new accommodations in compliance with the SPCA Order," I said.

"He's not here," said Mankle. "I got rid of him. Where the heck were you yesterday?"

We pushed our way past Mankle and down the stairs to the basement—no Zuma. Back upstairs, a sleepy looking Jeff Richardson emerged from the bedroom and declared, "There are no animals living in my house anymore."

We went outside and looked in the garage—nothing but typical yard junk in the garage. As I stood there gathering my thoughts and wondering where the animal could be, my eyes fell on Mankle's rusty old van parked on the street. "Is it just me, or is that van moving?" I said to no one in particular. I picked up my pace and headed for the van.

When I peered in the back window, I was shocked to see Zuma chained on no more that 10 inches (25 cm) of chain to the inside wall of the van. All the windows and doors were shut tight, but not locked.

"It must be 100 degrees in there," said Dr. Royle.

"Right. Now I have my grounds to remove an animal that is clearly in immediate distress" I said. "Let's get the drugs ready to tranquilize him. I only need the pole syringe, not the dart gun, for this."

Dr. Royle prepared the solution and handed me the pole syringe. Zuma jumped when I jabbed him with the injection but soon laid down in the van. I was sure he was secure, although not anesthetized yet, but I had to get some air in there quickly. I started opening doors and windows. In anticipation of what I knew would be a few minutes before Zuma was good and sleepy, I started my little SPCA station wagon and put the air conditioning on full blast.

After about 20 minutes, Dr. Royle gave Zuma a poke in the rump with the other end of the pole syringe and declared it safe to approach him. She gave the cat a quick physical exam, made sure his airway was clear and helped me load Zuma into my car.

All the while, the police officer watched and was suitably impressed with the efficiency and speed that the good doctor and I worked. Dr. Royle sat in my car with the doors locked while I returned to the house with the police officer and served Mr. Paul Mankle with his notice of removal. "What the … is this," was all he said as I pressed the standard form into his hand.

Mankle and Richardson had been so busy trying to make their morning coffee that they hadn't noticed Zuma being seized from the van on the street.

One other benefit from my previous zoo experience is that I have kept a good relationship with several of the better small private zoos in the province. Within two hours, Zuma was waking up in a secure, clean, suitable cougar cage at a proper zoo.

When Mankle had finally had his morning coffee and regained most of his senses—around four that afternoon—he called the office and unleashed a stream of profanity on poor Maud. Maud, with class and dignity, quietly said, "Sir, I am a lady, and I don't have to listen to such language, so. … off to you too," whereupon Maud put the phone down and went about her business.

I had hoped that Mankle would do nothing, and when the legal time period had passed, I could adopt Zuma to his new zoo custodians. No such luck.

On the fourth day after the removal, I received notice that Mankle had exercised his rights and launched an appeal to the provincial Animal Care Review Board. A date was set for the hearing, and Dr. Royle and I headed downtown. Mankle was already there, wearing a suit that I'm sure he had borrowed, hair slicked down, scruffy beard shaved off and smelling like he had done several laps in a pool of Old Spice aftershave lotion. Richardson was there as well, and much to my surprise, so was the police officer who had unleashed the stream of verbal abuse on Mankle.

"Why are you here?" I said to the officer.

"That nut bar subpoenaed me. Can you believe that?" he said as he gestured toward Mankle.

We each gave our evidence, were questioned by the SPCA corporate lawyer and then cross-examined by Mankle. Mankle acted as his own lawyer and gave evidence in his own defense.

Some people think that the role of the Animal Care Review Board is to determine guilt or innocence. Their function is actually to determine if the animal in question was in distress as defined in the SPCA Act and if the SPCA officer acted properly in terms of the Act. The board will also order the disposition of the animal to go back to the owner, once the distress has been relieved and specific conditions have been met. The board cannot deny a person the ownership of their animal.

I kept thinking of the old adage "A person who represents himself as counsel has a fool for a lawyer." This sure was a good example of that.

The chair of the board had to interrupt and correct Mankle several times during the day, but the best part was when Mankle called the police officer to the witness stand. The officer's testimony was frank and honest and clearly not what Mankle had expected.

The board ruled that the animal was indeed in distress and that the SPCA had acted properly in removing the animal. The board advised Mankle that he could have his animal back just as soon as he provided the proper and suitable cougar cage described in the original Order and after he paid all of the costs incurred by the SPCA in caring for his animal.

The general public usually sees this as a flaw in law or mistake on the part of the board, but I saw those decisions as a victory. We were correct in what we did and how we did it—we relieved the distress of the animal. The animal can go back because in the eyes of the law an animal is an item of property, but the distress must continue to be relieved and the bill must be paid.

Mankle spent much of the time during the hearing looking at the door. He expected the media to arrive at any moment and he would get some of that much-coveted free publicity. None came.

I suspect that when Paul Mankle went to his parents for one more loan of cash to pay his debt to the SPCA and buy materials to build a cougar cage, he found that their generosity had stopped.

We never heard from Mankle again, and there was little point in pursuing him through small claims court for the money he owed the SPCA—one more bill absorbed by the SPCA. Thank goodness for generous financial supporters.

The last time I saw Zuma, he was living a pretty happy life with another cougar for company in a proper zoo.

Pomeranians!

Early in my career, I had been promoted to the position of branch manager at the Whitby Branch of the OSPCA. The branch no longer exists, and the municipality now performs the animal control function. In the 1970s and early '80s, the OSPCA had the contract to provide animal control services. We also enforced the animal cruelty legislation, the OSPCA Act.

Although I was the Manager, I still took a turn at being on call for emergencies. As luck would have it, I was the person on call on a Friday evening around seven when a call for assistance came from the Durham Regional Police.

The police dispatcher asked if we covered the area east of the city of Oshawa, and did I know where Mitchells Corners was? As it happened, I had driven through Mitchells Corners several times and knew how to get there.

The dispatcher was very relieved, as she had been calling various other agencies and none would or could come to assist the police. She went on to ask me if I knew where the "hole in the wall" was. I did not, but she explained that I should drive north from the four corners and I would see a railroad bridge that looks like it was carved out of a brick wall, just wide enough for one car. If I continued driving north, I would soon see several police vehicles on the west side of the road.

The dispatcher couldn't tell me much but said I would need a lot of cages and that I would be dealing with a number of dogs.

The animal shelter was on my way, so I stopped and loaded as many dog crates as I could fit in my full-sized SPCA van and double-checked that I had other emergency equipment.

Although Mitchells Corners was outside of our animal control area, we covered a larger region when it came to cruelty calls, and assisting the police was always a priority call.

The directions from the dispatcher were impeccable. When I arrived at the scene, it looked like there had been a major disaster. A total of four police cruisers and an ambulance were scattered across the front lawn and driveway of a semi-rural lot that had a small, single-story house on it. All of the emergency vehicles had their flashing lights on and several had floodlights trained on the house.

The officer in charge, Constable McNab, met me at my van and introduced himself. After the usual exchange of business cards and brief notes in our respective duty notebooks, McNab began to fill me in on the situation.

"The manager of the meat department at the local grocery store called us to advise that he had not seen the occupant of this house for several weeks," McNab said. "The butcher tells us that the lady comes to the store every day and gets free scraps of meat and bones to help feed her dogs. Sometimes the butcher will deliver the scraps if he has too much for her to carry. The last time he saw her was Thursday or Friday, two weeks ago. She was pretty sick, coughing up blood, and seemed very weak."

McNab went on to say that the lady was described as 5 foot, 2 inches tall (157 cm), 110 pounds (50 kg), about seventy years old. He felt that since there was no response to knocks at the door that she was either gravely ill or perhaps deceased. Therefore, they (and I) could enter the building without a warrant under exigent circumstances.

"The problem is," McNab stated, "there are a ton of dogs in there, and they won't let us in. We want you to go in, search for the old lady and then confine or remove the dogs."

Great. Me all alone with "a ton of dogs" to remove. Most police officers are not dog people and their size, uniform and related equipment attached to their belts make most animals uneasy at best and terrified in some cases.

I asked McNab to please have all of the flashing lights turned off and only one spotlight to illuminate the front door of the house.

I grabbed my trusty catch-pole (a tubular piece of equipment with a cable noose running through it) to help protect me and to possibly start catching dogs. The plastic flashlight kept behind the driver's seat of my van blinked a couple of times then went dark—nice. Dead batteries. I made a mental note to buy new batteries the next day.

McNab handed me his flashlight, and after putting on my coveralls and rubber boots, I headed for the house.

Oddly enough, there was no barking, even when I knocked on the door. But as soon as I opened the door, I could see several pairs of eyes staring back at me—Pomeranians! Small, fluffy, reddish-colored dogs, often referred to as lap dogs.

I half turned in the doorway and spoke over my shoulder to McNab, who was about three paces behind me with his hand on his gun. "They're just little dogs—Pomeranians," I said.

"Yeah, but watch what happens when you get right in there," was McNab's reply, "and remember, we want you to look for the old lady first."

Confident in my dog handling abilities, I turned back to the house, stepped in and closed the door behind me. I found a light switch, and to my surprise the hydro worked. Suddenly the room was lit up.

Imagine what a single kernel of popcorn feels like when all the other kernels are popping. That is what flashed through my mind. Pomeranians too numerous to count were bouncing off the walls, shooting under furniture, leaving the room and returning just as fast. "Holy crap!" I said, a term that seems to come to me before any other and is sometimes blurted out at the most inappropriate times. It seemed entirely appropriate this time.

The dogs were not trying to attack me but were frantic to get away from me.

I slowly walked through the rest of the living room area, which was cluttered with basic furniture—a couch, two large arm chairs, TV trays, a TV stand and old television set, a couple of floor lamps—and lots of dog feces on everything. There were articles of clothing, newspapers, magazines, empty dog food bags, butcher's wrapping paper and other litter strewn throughout the entire house. No windows were open, and the air hung thick, damp and moldy.

To my left was a small kitchen also littered with feces, the same junk, and a table and four chairs, fridge, stove, sink and cupboards. To the right was a bedroom with its door jammed open by all of the junk in there. I could see a double bed, dresser, other small cabinets and an antique steamer trunk.

Through the kitchen, I could see the back door, which opened into the back yard, a closed door that I assumed and later confirmed was the bathroom, and no other doors to other rooms except a closed closet door in the bedroom. As I was slowly walking into the bedroom to look in the closet, the dogs, which I now estimated to number around thirty, were still bouncing off the walls in their efforts to stay away from me. I cleared the junk away from the bottom of the closet door with my booted foot and opened the door.

The entire closet was jammed with ladies' clothes that looked like they would fit a person as described by the butcher to Constable McNab. As I was slowly walking through the house, I was calling out, "Anybody here?" I could feel the hairs on the back of my neck standing straight up, not from fear of the dogs (clearly they were more afraid of me), but because I expected to find a very sick person hiding, or even a dead body.

"No little old lady in there," I proclaimed to McNab as I emerged from the house, eager to inhale some fresh air.

I backed my van up to the front door of the house and placed three or four crates on the front steps. I knew that my catch-pole was not going to be needed, so I grabbed my thick leather welder's gloves and a net from the van.

Now poised in the middle of the living room, I was able to scoop flying Pomeranians in my net as they bounced off the walls. A good grip on the scruff of the neck and into a kennel crate they went. Where I thought two would fit and get along, I put two per crate and placed the full crate out on the steps, taking in another empty crate.

The ambulance had departed, having heard that there were no sick or dying people in the house. When the other officers got a whiff of the house, most of them suddenly had other calls to attend. Only Constable McNab and his partner remained, and they were very helpful in stacking the crates full of dogs in my van and handing me empty cages.

It was around midnight when I was sure that all of the dogs were out of the house. The two police officers did a walk through with me; still no body to be found.

"We will secure this scene and check the hospitals and canvass the neighbourhood," said McNab. "But I suspect we will be back in here to do a more thorough search in the daylight tomorrow."

I locked my van and opened the windows to get some fresh air. I'm sure the dogs were as grateful as I for that. After I made some notes in my duty notebook, I headed back to the Whitby animal shelter, where I moved a few resident animals and emptied one kennel room that would accommodate all of the 28 Pomeranians. I left some notes of explanation for the kennel staff and, after giving the dogs some food and water, headed for home.

Monday morning I was surprised to see one of the kennel attendants petting one of the Pomeranians. She had worked over the weekend and found that the dogs were very frightened, but none showed any signs of aggression.

I started my paperwork and put the usual legal notices in the mail to the owner at the last known address so that we could resolve the issue of ownership as quickly as possible and perhaps get the Pomeranians into foster homes or adopt them to new permanent homes.

Late Tuesday afternoon, I was getting ready to leave the shelter when the phone rang and the receptionist handed me the phone. "It's Constable McNab for you," she said.

"Hugh Coghill," I said.

"Hey, she was in there," said officer McNab.

"Get out!" I said. My mind quickly ran through the events of last Friday and searched again every part of that house. How could we have missed a human being in the midst of that rubble?

McNab went on, "Do you remember the old streamer trunk in the bedroom?"

"Yes."

"Well, there was a pink laundry basket on top of the trunk, and in the basket were some articles of clothing and a piece of triangular bone that we knew was too big to be from a dead dog. So four of us spent the day on Saturday throwing everything out on the front lawn, piece by piece, and we discovered a bunch of bones. We took the bones down to the forensic lab at the coroner's office in Toronto. He just called me to say that we had the bones of three dogs and one elderly human."

"Holy crap!" There it is again—oops.

McNab said the coroner couldn't determine cause of death, but the likely scenario was that she collapsed and died in the house shortly after the time the butcher saw her spitting up blood. When the dogs got hungrier and hungrier, they eventually saw her as food and started to eat her. Clearly, three of their buddies also perished and got eaten as well.

"I mean, they picked her clean. There wasn't even hair or fingernails left, just clean bones." McNab sounded astounded at the whole thing.

I asked if the police had found any relatives of the old lady, and he told me that she was all alone in this world, no relatives. Her last will and testament, also found in the house, indicated her desire to leave all her worldly belongings to the Catholic church.

The office of the public guardian would look after the dispersal of the assets. I was apparently clear to put the dogs up for adoption, pending a veterinary health check.

The police have their own public relations department, and they must have issued a press release, because the local newspapers all carried the tragic story on the front page—some with pretty graphic details.

The following day, I received a phone call from one of our major supporters asking for my assurances that all of those poor little dogs would be placed into loving new homes. "After all," the caller said, "they have been through a traumatic ordeal, and we owe it to them to find new homes."

Not long after that call, a man called and demanded that all of the dogs be destroyed immediately. "Once they taste human flesh, they crave it for life!"

What a load of garbage. If you transposed that line of thinking to proper dog food, you would assume that dogs will always chase horses, or cows or whatever other meat source that they have been given.

But logic didn't seem to enter into this dilemma. More and more people were calling to express their sentiments for or against adoption.

Being a relatively new branch manager, I felt the need to get some direction from higher up and called the CEO at the provincial office.

After I explained the scenario and my dilemma, his response was, "You're the manager—manage!" Then he hung up the phone.

I advised staff to inform future callers that the dogs were not up for adoption at this time, but they could check back in a few days.

I had a few days of turmoil while I tried to decide what to do with these little dogs, but fate made the decision for me.

Back in the early 1980s, parvovirus was a very serious problem disease in animal shelters. There was no vaccine for the disease, and treatment was costly. The disease was often fatal, with very unpleasant symptoms.

By Friday of that week, we started having bloody diarrhea in the dogs. We called the local vet, who was also on the board of directors of the Whitby Branch.

He stepped into the kennel room, took a deep breath, saw the diarrhea and turned to me and said, "Euthanize them all."

In fact, he insisted that we do the deed immediately in order to end their suffering. We had to remove every piece of equipment, food/water bowls, etc., and sanitize the room.

All equipment and staff were to leave boots and coveralls at the shelter in order to protect their own animals as well as the dogs in the rest of the shelter.

It was fortunate that we had kept these dogs isolated from the rest of the shelter but also tragic that their first time leaving the home with the old lady was to an animal control shelter where they were exposed to a deadly disease.

Thirty-five years later, every time I see a Pomeranian, my mind still casts back to those poor little dogs.

Mr. Peebottle

During my lengthy career in animal welfare, I have seen a lot of great people come and go.

Most people get into the business because they have a compassion for animals and hate to see them abused or neglected. Many leave the field because of those very same deep, passionate feelings.

Some folks see things through rose-colored lenses. When the stark reality hits them, they can't take the emotional ups and downs. There has also always been an odd political culture in the animal welfare business, making the job even more difficult to endure.

I recall when I managed one of the local shelters many years ago; there was a wonderful lady who worked as a kennel attendant. She truly loved animals and always went above and beyond her regular duties to try to find homes for all the animals in our care.

One day she came to work and asked to meet with me in private. She soon burst into tears and announced her resignation. Unknown to me and the rest of the staff, she had been seeing a psychiatrist to try to overcome her emotional turmoil in dealing with the issue of euthanasia. When the cost of her doctor's appointments exceeded her income, her husband insisted that the job had to go. I never saw her again.

When I began my work life in the late 1970s, it was in an SPCA facility that provided animal control services for several municipalities. After the legal redemption period, the dogs and cats went up for adoption, but the dozen or so kennels and several dozen cat cages were not nearly enough to handle the flow of animals. Killing surplus animals to create much-needed space was a stark reality.

This wasn't euthanasia—mercy killing to end suffering. This was killing healthy, happy animals because more were on their way every single day. Often a dozen cats and six to 10 dogs were killed in a week. In those days, the method of euthanasia was far less humane than what we have available to us now. Fortunately, the numbers of animal killed seems to have constantly declined, and the methods used have greatly improved. In many areas now, animals are only put to death if they are suffering or if they have serious behavioural issues that cannot be remediated. Animals are also transferred to other shelters in an effort to relieve local overcrowding.

In the investigation department, we attracted people with a law enforcement background or an animal husbandry background. In either case, they always declared their love of animals and a desire to protect animals and punish offenders.

As with the shelter staff, many were soon overcome with disillusion. Animals that were seized from a neglectful owner, brought back to good health, then ordered returned to the same owner by a judicial board or the courts were a constant cause of frustration. The proverbial slap on the wrist from the court as punishment for the most heinous acts of cruelty or neglect was another source of angst, and we lost more good people.

Few people seemed to stick it out for the long haul and persevere in the quest to help animals for decades of their working lives, but Millie Harris was one of those people.

When Millie left animal welfare, at the same time that I left the provincial SPCA, she was just one week short of 20 years of service to the cause.

Millie was an inspector and I was chief inspector when she dropped by my office one hot July afternoon. She knew that despite my never-ending workload, I would want to hear about the call that she and Officer Manse had been to. Sandra Manse was the brightest and keenest rising star among our staff that I had seen in a few years. Sandra had an incredible ability to immediately assess an individual, often in highly charged, emotional situations and calmly work to deescalate a situation by trying to see all sides of the equation.

Sandra received the initial call from the local police and asked Millie if she could assist her on what may turn out to be a feral cat round-up.

They arrived at the house on the edge of King City to find police, fire, hydro, municipal bylaw and property standards people already on the property.

One look around at the scene of uniformed men tromping in and around the house and emergency vehicles with lights flashing and Sandra calmly said to Millie, "Any chance of finding any cats here today have certainly disappeared. These guys sure don't make our job any easier, and they sure as heck don't know the first thing about animals."

The police officer in charge noted the arrival of the SPCA truck and headed over to greet Sandra and Millie. After the formal exchange of business cards, quick notes in duty note books, describing location, arrival times and names of others present, the police officer advised that there had been a small fire at the house earlier in the day.

An elderly gentleman had been taken by the authorities for a psychiatric assessment. It seems that when the fire department arrived in response to a 911 call placed by a concerned citizen who noticed smoke coming from the house, they were horrified at what they saw.

After climbing through massive heaps of litter in the house, the firemen were able to douse the flames but felt there was a high risk of new fires because of all the junk piled so close to the electrical panel in the house.

Police usually attend when there is a fire, and they called the local hydroelectric company to come and shut off the service to the house to reduce the risk of fire.

After a look through the house, the police decided that no one in their right mind would live like that. They called an ambulance to come and get Mr. Broist. Broist didn't seem to understand what all the fuss was about, but he was very concerned for his cats. Who would look after them? The police assured him that the SPCA would look after the cats.

Sandra explained to the officer that any cats still on the property would almost certainly be in hiding, so the best they could do for now was to make sure there was plenty of food and water bowls out for the animals. They would place a notice on the door for the owner, or anyone else who may attend at the house, to call the SPCA for further information. This non-official notice card was referred to by SPCA staff as a **WYWO** (*wee-whoa*) card, which stands for "while you were out." It's simply meant to inform the owner/tenant who it is that has been on their property during their absence.

The police officer assured the two SPCA officers that this owner was "going away for a long time," but we had heard that many times before.

Millie, now cooling off from the outside heat and sitting in my office, said she expected the owner would be out in a day or so. She and Sandra didn't see any cats, but they made sure there was lots of food and water in the house. The unique thing with this house was that the junk piled throughout was mostly plastic bottles, all containing some amount of liquid. The bottles filled every room of the house, piled in heaps up to two meters high, leaving little less than a small pathway through the entire house. Room after room was full of half-empty soda pop bottles, water bottles, juice bottles, all sorts of plastic bottles and the occasional glass jar. All had some fluid in them and were tightly closed with their respective lids.

Millie couldn't offer any explanation for the situation but made the comment, "Just when you think you've seen everything ..." as she left my office with the promise to keep me posted on this one.

The following day, Sandra received a call from a soft-spoken gentleman who identified himself as Calvin Broist. He had spent the night in the hospital, but was fine now, having been released very early that morning. He had returned home to find the SPCA note on his door. He had walked the one-kilometer trek to the local variety store in order to use the pay phone, not having a phone of his own.

Sandra arranged for a time that she and Millie could return to meet Mr. Broist and discuss his cats.

When they arrived at the Broist home later that same day, Calvin was standing in the driveway with one of his beloved cats in his arms—a beautiful slate-grey cat quite content to be cuddled by the owner. Two other cats wove between his legs as he stood there waiting for the SPCA to arrive.

When the two cats on the ground spotted Millie and Sandra emerging from their truck, they made a hasty retreat to the safety of the bottle-strewn house. The grey cat in his arms was alert and wary of the approaching strangers, but stayed with Broist the whole time of the SPCA visit.

After the usual pleasantries were exchanged, Calvin invited the two officers to see the rest of his cats, now inside the house. The three people and one cat had to move in single file as they wove through the mountain of bottles, until they reached the kitchen. Broist, speaking softly, assured his little friends that the strange people were good people and meant them no harm. Sandra and Millie exchanged a quick glance at each other and both said "six" at the same time. Broist heard them and confirmed that he did indeed own six cats—all fully vaccinated, all neutered and all in good health.

Although Broist had worked his entire adult life as a construction labourer and paid off his mortgage several years ago, his only income now was the government pension. He admitted that he had difficulty keeping up with his bills.

Broist boasted, "When I bought this house, King City was just a little stagecoach stop on the way from Toronto to Barrie. Now look at it! I can hardly keep up with the taxes, let alone pay for hydro and buy food for me and my kitties."

Broist went on to tell them that he had been married, but he and "the missus" never had kids, so they always took in the local stray cats, had them fixed and fed as many as they could afford. His wife of over 50 years had passed away nearly a decade ago, but he stayed in the home, and now, at nearly 80 years old, he was finding things a little tough.

Sandra and Mille commended Calvin on the good health of the cats and promised to drop by in a couple of days to see how he was doing. "If you're passing that Tim Horton's down the road when you come back, mines a double double," was

Calvin's parting comment. Like many Canadians, Calvin loved his Tim Horton's coffee.

A few kilometers down the road, on the way back to the office, Millie looked in the rear view mirror to see the flashing lights of a police car. After a few harsh words in anger (Millie had what we called a lead foot), she pulled over and reached for the ownership, insurance and her driver's licence.

When she opened the driver's window and handed her documents out, she was pleased to see the same officer from the day before at the Broist house.

"Put that away," said the cop. He pointed back towards the Broist house. "I saw you in there and just wanted to know what was happening with the cats. I'm a cat lover myself, you know."

Millie told the officer that the animals appeared to be in good condition, so there was nothing that the SPCA could or would want to do, except to encourage him to clean the place up a little.

"Anyway, you told me he was going away for a long time. What happened?" Millie said.

"Apparently, if you are no danger to yourself or to others, they can't keep you, so he got out this morning. If he can clean the place up a little, his hydro will get switched back on," said the officer.

Millie kept me apprised of this ongoing situation, and we agreed that she should take a few dollars out of our staff cash pot for the office coffee to buy Broist a coffee and a bagel or muffin each time they went back. Broist was very grateful each time and would rummage around his empty pockets in an effort to find some money to pay for the treat. None would be found, but he would savour every drop of that cup of coffee and eat his bagel or muffin as if it was a gift from heaven.

Even though he was a well-spoken gentleman, there was clearly something odd going on in his mind. It was agreed that two officers would always attend.

After a half dozen regular visits, coffee in hand, as well as some surplus cat food and litter from the shelter, Millie finally got around to asking him what it was with all the bottles and what was in them?

"Well," said Broist, "you see, I'm under doctor's orders."

"Doctor's orders? I don't understand," said Millie.

"About five years ago, the doctor handed me a little bottle and told me to pee in it, so I did, and have ever since."

Apparently the doctor's request for a urine sample was misunderstood to be an order to pee in bottles from then on—which he did.

All of those bottles were full or half full of Calvin Broist's urine over a five-year period. No one had told him to stop.

By the time Millie and Sandra had returned to the office, they had coined his nickname, "Mr. Peebottle." Once a week or so, I offered some money to help pay for a cup of coffee and a bagel for Mr. Peebottle.

Old Farmer's Syndrome

I have great respect for farmers, having dabbled in several aspects of farming during my life and also having worked on several other farms to gain experience and knowledge.

However, there is an interesting situation that crops up from time to time, and I have often said that someday a psychology student will do some research and write a thesis, perhaps calling it "Old Farmer's Syndrome."

It may be that this kind of thinking exists in other types of businesses, but I have only seen it with farmers.

Farmers work long, hard hours every day of the year. If a farmer has made agriculture his life's work, he may do this for three, four, five or even more decades.

Sometimes, the lifelong farmer truly believes that he can still perform the work at the same level he did when he was 20 years old, even though he may be 70 or 80 years old.

Such was the case with Percy Harris, or as it stated on his driver's license (examined for identification purposes), Percival James Harris. His driver's license also indicated that he was 78 years of age.

Max and I decided to leave our SPCA vehicle at the road and approached the house on foot through knee-deep snow. Mr. Harris emerged from his house with two five-gallon pails full of water, stopped on the steps of his house and peered at the two uniformed officers trudging through the snow to meet him. The odd thing with Mr. Harris was that one leg was much shorter than the other. When he put his pails of water down, he stood there talking to us while balancing on the longer of his two legs, reminiscent of a flamingo resting on one leg.

Max asked Harris what he was doing with the pails of water, and he said it was for the cows. We offered to carry the water for him, but he insisted that it gave him balance and he preferred to carry them himself. He was happy to show us his cows, but as we walked the hundred or so meters to the barn, he was explaining that the pump for the barn water had frozen and he was carrying the water down from the house—every day.

I asked how many cows he had and after a long pause, he said, "Hmmmm, oh, I guess around ninety head."

Knowing that cattle need approximately 1 US gallon of water for each 100 pounds of body weight (3.78 liters/45 Kg) and a mix of adult cows and growing heifers would probably have an average weight of 600 to 800 pounds of body weight, it was very clear that one man with two five-gallon pails couldn't possibly carry enough water for 90 animals, even if he worked non-stop 24 hours a day.

In my mind, we were heading for a barn that housed a disaster.

Our original call regarding the Harris farm was from a man who would not leave his name, but he was pretty sure that Percy had a number of dead animals in his barn.

The SPCA does respond to anonymous calls, but if we are denied entry, it is difficult, if not impossible, to get a search warrant based on an anonymous call. Fortunately, Mr. Harris was quite happy to show us his cattle.

As we approached the barn, we could hear the sounds of many cows mooing. When Percy opened the door, a gust of warm, steamy air rushed out at us and assaulted our sense of smell. Rotting corpses have a very distinct aroma. Once you have had that smell in your nose, you never forget it. I have been told by several police officers that a decaying human corpse gives off the exact same odour; in fact, any decomposing body has the same, or very similar odour.

At this point, I was glad that Max and I had agreed to have an early start this day. I was now sure we would be here for quite some time.

Having seen several dead animals just inside the door and the very thin condition of the few live animals visible from the door, Max excused himself and stepped back outside to use his cell phone. Once inside the barn with the door closed, it took a few seconds for my eyes to adjust to the dim lighting. I could not walk more that a meter in any direction without having to step on or climb over the body of a dead cow.

Among the dead were many live animals, but they all seemed to be very thin, weak and tired from also having to climb over the bodies of their herd mates as they searched for scraps of hay and a place at the empty water trough.

When an animal dies, the contents of the gut continue to ferment and create gas. This is especially evident with ruminant animals such as cattle. When the gas finally finds a way to escape from the rotting body, the resulting stench is truly gut-wrenching.

Percy, however, could see the good side of this fact. He kept the doors closed in order to keep the heat in the barn, in hopes that the frozen water system would rectify itself.

I continued to wander through the barn with Mr. Harris and started to count the dead and live animals as we picked our way over and around bodies of partially decomposed animals.

Percy was explaining to me that he had farmed right here at this location for over fifty years. His wife had passed away some time ago, and the kids were all grown up and moved away. He found that about ninety head was a good number and had kept his herd of mixed-breed beef cattle around that number for all those years, shipping about forty to fifty fat heifers and steers each fall.

We emerged from the barn at the other end of the building after Percy had dumped his two buckets into a trough and several animals pushed their way to the trough to get a drink. The blinding sunlight and cold, wintery-fresh air were a welcome relief. Percy said there were a few more animals upstairs that had been loose in the barnyard but had broken into the hay mow in search of food. At this point, my count of dead animals was at 40.

When Percy opened up the big doors of the upper level of the barn, we discovered about a dozen animals gorging themselves on the hay. Unfortunately, the floor of the old barn wasn't too good, and four animals had broken through with their legs dangling below them They were a sad sight to see.

Max rejoined us and pulled me aside to tell me that he had a veterinarian and a livestock transportation company on their way. "I told them about ninety head of cattle—is that correct?" asked Max. I told him that the number would be less than 50 and questioned how we were going to get the cattle up to the road when the trucks arrived, since the snow was deep enough, and the slope down to the barn steep enough, that no truck would be able to navigate it.

Max called the trucking company back to adjust the numbers and ignored my question about the snow.

I turned my attention back to Percy Harris and told him that we had a vet on the way and that it was very likely we would be taking his cows away. I asked if he had any family or friends that he could call to come over to be with him, knowing that this was going to be a devastating day for him.

Percy responded by saying that he had no friends or family in the immediate area, and if we took his cattle away, he would simply go out and buy more. This was an issue that we would have to address later. At this point, I was still worried about his mental state and how this situation would affect him.

The veterinarian arrived in about a half hour, greeted Percy on a first name basis, and asked what the problem was. Percy told him that a couple of animals had died and he hadn't been able to get the bodies out. He also explained that he had to carry water down from the house by hand since the water pump or the water line in the barn was frozen.

The vet turned to me and said, "When you have livestock, you will have deadstock. You people in the SPCA need to understand that." With that, the vet opened the barn door and stepped inside. When I saw the look on his face, I so wanted to make a sarcastic comment about what level of deadstock he thought we should understand, but I bit my tongue and let him express his shock and utter disgust.

The vet turned to Mr. Harris and said, "Percy, I told you a long time ago, you needed to reduce the size of your herd and your workload."

Percy's response was, "I've always had about ninety cattle. I can cope with that workload."

I advised the vet that it was my intention to remove the live animals from the farm in order to take them to a place where they could receive proper care and husbandry, but that it would be helpful to me if he agreed. He indicated that there was no other option in his mind, and further, there were a total of five animals that he would certify to be humanely destroyed as they could not possibly be cured or healed enough to live productive lives. The five animals included the four that had broken through the floor as well as one that I had counted as dead in the lower part of the barn but was actually still alive and being trampled by the other animals.

Our conversation was interrupted by the sound of the largest John Deere tractor I have ever seen backing down the laneway, blowing the snow and creating a clear path as it crept ever closer to us at the barn.

Apparently a neighbor had seen the SPCA vehicle at the road, and word got around the neighbourhood very fast. The farmer with the tractor just lived a couple of miles down the road and figured we needed some help. He stopped the tractor when he got close to us and opened the cab door to tell us that some of the other neighbours were also coming by to not only help us, but to bring Percy some food and stay with him for a while.

My faith in humanity just jumped up a notch. I turned to Percy to make sure he heard that comment as well. Percy had his head down, and I could see he was trying to hide his tears.

Max retrieved the Accles & Shelvoke Captive Bolt pistol that we carried in our vehicle, and the five distressed animals were put out of their misery. A captive bolt pistol is the instrument used in many slaughter facilities to render an animal unconscious so that it can be hoisted and bled out before being cut up. The pistol does not fire a projectile, but forces a steel bolt into the brain of the animal, instantly knocking the animal unconscious. Because it does not fire a projectile, it isn't considered a firearm and can be carried without special permits.

A livestock tractor-trailer as well as a smaller livestock truck soon arrived. The drivers decided they would keep the tractor-trailer out on the road where they knew they wouldn't get stuck and use the smaller truck to load about a dozen animals at a time and ferry them out to the other vehicle.

This was a fairly slow process, since most of the animals were very weak and some needed help negotiating the ramp onto the truck.

When we were finally finished we had a head count of 45 live animals, 40 dead and five euthanized by us, for a total of 90 animals—exactly what Percy had said.

I served Mr. Percival James Harris with the appropriate paperwork and left him in the comfort of his home with several neighbours who thanked me and said they would stay with Percy for a few days.

Once settled in to the SPCA farm, with deep straw bedding, the cattle were gradually rehydrated and fed back to a normal state over several days, and they began to flourish and gain weight.

Percy did not appeal the seizure of his animals, and they were sold by auction several weeks later.

The quandary I had was how to keep this kind, old farmer from going out and buying more cattle and falling into the same difficult position again. Sadly, the only answer was that I had to lay a charge under the Criminal Code and, if he were convicted, ask the court to prohibit Mr. Harris from owning cattle for as long as legally possible.

About two months after the cattle were taken from Mr. Harris, I was on my way to the Harris farm to give Percy a cheque for the proceeds of the sale of his cattle, minus the SPCA's costs, but also to serve him with a summons to court to answer to the charge of neglecting his cattle.

When I arrived at the farm, the laneway had been kept clear of snow, and tracks indicated that lots of vehicles had come and gone in recent days. As I exited my vehicle, I stopped and listened. Not a sound could be heard—no cattle, no other animals, not even a bird singing in a tree. It was one of those very quiet, sunny, late winter days when it seems like everything has paused to listen for the sounds of the arrival of spring.

A man exiting the house with a box in his hands broke the silence.

I asked for Mr. Harris and the man put the box down, shook my hand and said, "I'm Jim Harris."

After explaining who I was and what I was doing there, he advised me that Percy was his father. When he and other family members heard what had happened, they became more involved in Percy's life. He told me that his father was now living in a retirement home in town. They had all the dead animals removed and were cleaning up the house and barn so the property could be sold. He said that Percy had been fitted with a special orthopedic shoe to level the length of his legs, and he could now walk without a limp.

Sadly, this action could only take place after the family doctor had certified that Mr. Harris was suffering from dementia. His farming days were now behind him.

Cleary there was no reason to proceed with the criminal charges, so on my way back to the office, I stopped at the courthouse. After explaining the situation to the Crown Attorney, he agreed to withdraw the charge.

Unfortunately, Percival James Harris is not unique. During my time working in animal welfare, both in Ontario and British Columbia, I have encountered several other old farmers who were trying to cope with the same workload they did when they were in their 20s, all with similar disastrous results. I always tried to get family members involved and see if a more compassionate solution to the Old Farmer Syndrome could be found.

The Wolf Sanctuary—Part One

The OSPCA was going through a transitional period when I was appointed as the acting chief inspector. We also had an acting CEO while the Provincial Board of Directors made some strategic decisions regarding the structure and future of the organization.

For me and the rest of the Investigation Department, we just carried on as usual, doing our jobs, working within the framework of the existing structure and the parameters of the SPCA Act.

On one of those wintery Saturday nights where you just got snuggled into your warm bed for a good night's sleep, one of our officers received a call from an Ontario Provincial Police officer requesting assistance.

The officer described an unpleasant scene that he and his partner had discovered when they responded to a domestic violence call in a rural area of Eastern Ontario.

The officer advised that this call was unusual in several ways: first, the victim was a male person who had been battered by his now-estranged female partner. Second, the officers had discovered that the female occupant was the owner of a young African lion.

While taking a statement from the victim in the kitchen, one of the officers happened to look up at the ceiling and observe a large, brown stain that had been creeping across the white ceiling. When he asked the male occupant what was causing that stain, the man said, "Oh, that's from the lion."

The officer returned to writing his statement, then suddenly looked back at the man and said, "Wait, did you say lion?"

The two officers knew they were in a rural area but had missed the small sign at the end of the laneway that said, "Welcome to the wolf sanctuary of eastern Ontario." They were not surprised to see several dogs and domestic cats in the house when they entered, but the many cages for other animals outside had escaped their attention, partly because it was dark outside and partly because their focus was on the house, where the victim and perpetrator were believed to be.

After asking to see the lion, the male victim of the alleged domestic violence escorted the police officer up the stairs, where they both peered into a dark, wire-fronted cage about half the size of the small bedroom. Inside the cage was a young lion that seemed to ignore their presence but also seemed intent on getting out of the cramped cage, which they estimated to be about 4 feet (1.2 meters) wide and 10 feet (3 meters) long. The bottom of the cage was littered with feces, old newspaper, a torn sofa cushion and a few bones, likely left over from meat being fed to the animal. The officer noted some scrapes on the nose of the big cat and asked the man why he had a lion.

The male victim indicated that all the animals belonged to his ex-girlfriend, who was being interviewed by the other officer downstairs.

Once his statement was recorded on paper, he signed it, gathered a duffle bag of clothes and left the house.

The perpetrator, now identified as Lillian Swinger, admitted that she had legally changed her name to Swinger about 20 years ago when she was an active employee of a local escort service. She was issued a promise to appear notice with a future court date for her to answer to the charge of common assault, and the police officers left the scene.

Once back at the station, the call was placed to the local SPCA officer.

Officer Rosemary Tandry (Rosie for short) advised the officer that she would be by the station in the morning to pick up a copy of the police report, as that would form the basis for her information to obtain a search warrant under the authority of the OSPCA Act. Once that warrant was obtained, she would request police assistance to execute the warrant.

Monday morning found Rosie at the courthouse, where the local justice of the peace was absolutely stunned to learn that someone had an African lion living right in his community.

Warrant in hand, Rosie headed for the wolf sanctuary with a police cruiser close behind her.

Swinger was in the middle of feeding her wolves when Tandry and the police arrived to see the lion. Swinger thought she could divert some of the attention away from the fact that she had a lion by showing officer Tandry and the police officer her wolves that she proclaimed to be the nucleus of a captive breeding program that was the envy of conservationists across Canada.

Rosie was not impressed. In fact, she took out an SPCA Order form from the clipboard she always carried with her while conducting a cruelty investigation and started writing up orders for Ms. Swinger to clean up the winter's worth of accumulated feces and leftover bones from the many carcasses of road-kill -deer and dead stock from the farmers in the area. Swinger was given a week to clean the place up, or the SPCA would return to remove the animals. Now she was really worried about showing Rosie her pet lion.

As the three of them worked their way up the stairs of the house, past the dogs and domestic cats that were running loose in the house, the stench of ammonia from cat urine was overwhelming to Rosie and the police officer. Swinger seemed oblivious.

After a quick look at the conditions in the house for the dogs, cats and the lion, Rosie took out another order form once again. This time, Swinger said, "Look, I didn't want the lion, my ex-boyfriend wanted it, and he has left now, so why don't you take the lion and put your order form away."

Rosie Tandry is one of the best field officers I have had the pleasure to know and work with, so when she was given the opportunity to get an animal out of a neglectful situation, she took it. She told Swinger that she didn't have a dog crate big enough or strong enough to hold a lion, but she did have a new home waiting for the cat. Rosie was always prepared. When she knew what she would be dealing with, she had put a call in to the provincial office. I made a few calls to people I knew in the zoo world in Ontario. A cage suitable for a lion was on standby at a central Ontario wildlife facility.

Swinger, eager to get rid of the lion and the scrutiny of the police and SPCA, offered to lend Tandry one of her steel wolf crates to transport the lion.

Tandry filled out the appropriate Surrender of Animal form and had Swinger sign it. She was given a copy, along with the several pages of OSPCA orders to clean the place up.

Once the crate was brought to the house, Swinger clipped a chain to the leather collar that was around the neck of her mostly tame lion and walked it right down the stairs and into the crate—easy as that!

I was about to head for home around 5:30 p.m. when my cell phone rang. It was officer Rosie Tandry, laughing so hard I could barely understand her. "Oh my gawd," she said "I have a lion in my truck, and I'm on my way up to the provincial office." Quite a change from the usual dog or cat that frequented the back of her truck.

My response? The usual: "Holy crap! I'll meet you at the wildlife facility just north of here. They have a cage ready to receive the lion."

Like most of the small zoos in Ontario, the wildlife facility is family-owned and -operated. When I called Dave, he and his wife were just finishing their dinner. He agreed to meet me at the service entrance to his facility. Dave is a soft-spoken, rather large, heavily bearded, mountain-man type of guy who is always willing to help out if he can.

As our truck headlights turned into his service entrance, he was unlocking the chain at the gate. He directed us to drive straight in and back up to the entry gate of the next large cage inside the facility. Dave told me that this cage was nearly a half-acre in size with no top on it, but there was an electric strand at the top of the 12-foot (4-meter) high fence, and all of the trees in the cage were wrapped with steel around the trunk so a cat could not climb them.

We wanted to remove the collar that Lillian Swinger had left around the lion's neck, so Dave perched himself on top of the cage. As I slid the sliding door open, he reached out, grabbed the collar and cut it with a pair of heavy tin snips in one swift movement. The lion simply walked straight out of the box and didn't even look up at Dave.

"She's pretty thin," said Dave, "and I think she is blind. See how she keeps walking into things?"

"That also explains the lesions on her nose," I said. She had been walking into the gate of her cage at Lillian's house.

We agreed to leave her to settle in with a large bowl of water and plenty of food for the night. Although it was still winter and below freezing overnight, the lion had a heated den to go into if she got cold.

Dave would arrange for his vet to come in the morning and check her out.

Tandry and I decided to meet at the coffee shop down the road so she could tell me about the rest of the wolf sanctuary.

The Wolf Sanctuary–Part Two

Officer Rosie Tandry did a couple of drive-by looks at the cages of the wolf sanctuary over the next week. It was pretty obvious that Ms. Swinger had made no effort to clean up any of the cages and that a removal of the animals was eminent.

Tandry had alerted me to this fact, and I had been actively calling zoos in Ontario and Quebec to find facilities that could board wolves, coyotes and foxes until the legal process was complete in the event that we had to remove the animals.

In addition, we had amassed enough large, strong crates to hold all of the animals and put a number of staff and their respective vehicles on alert to assist us should the operation go ahead.

When dealing with native wildlife, a call must also be placed to the local office of the Ministry of Natural Resources, or MNR. Some of our staff says that MNR stands for Ministry of No Response, due to their policy of leaving wildlife alone and not responding to calls of wild animals hit by cars on the road. However, when I called and said that we were in a position to seize all of the animals at the wolf sanctuary of eastern Ontario, they were very keen to become involved and make sure that the proper paperwork was completed to transfer these native animals to other registered facilities.

When the date of compliance of the OSPCA orders arrived, Tandry attended at the wolf sanctuary with Senior Inspector Granby.

Ms. Swinger was still in her nightgown, having her morning coffee, reading the local newspaper at her kitchen table when Tandry knocked on her door. When Tandry advised Swinger that she was there to ensure compliance with the order, Swinger simply said, "I don't care anymore. Take them all. I'll sign a surrender form right now." As usual, Rosie had a surrender form on her clipboard. She had Swinger list all of the animals at the sanctuary:

- 12 adult, purebred Timber wolves
- 4 hybrid wolf/dog crosses
- A pair of coyotes, imported from New York state
- A pair of red foxes
- Two raccoons
- One pony

Swinger would keep her pet dogs and cats that lived in the house.

Swinger admitted that the whole wolf sanctuary idea had been a dismal failure. She thought the local schools would send busloads of students there and pay her for the privilege of seeing the animals. She also thought that she could sell hybrid wolf/dogs to people via the Internet, but the MNR had informed her that this was illegal and would place her permit to keep the wolves in jeopardy.

Swinger had relied on the local farmers to drop off their dead stock, which she fed to the wolves and coyotes by simply dumping the whole carcasses into the animal pens. The smaller animals were fed cheap dog kibble that Swinger bought at the local farm supply store.

Tandry advised Swinger that she and several other SPCA staff would return the following day to remove all of the surrendered animals. Tandry also suggested that it might be a good idea for Swinger to leave for the day but that it was her right to be present if she wanted to be.

By 10:00 a.m., Rosie was on her cell phone to me to advise that the removal was a go and provide me with a final list of all the animals. She would arrange for a local horse farm to bring a trailer and take the pony.

After I made a few phone calls to put the final phases of the plan in place and set things in motion for the following day, I headed down the hall to the office of the acting CEO to brief him. This time it was his turn to say, "Holy crap!" as his face drained to an ashen white hue.

After I assured him that we had suitable zoo homes for most of the animals and that the raccoons and foxes would go to our wildlife rehabilitation facility in central Ontario, the colour returned to his face.

He asked me to keep him informed of our progress the next day, to make sure all of our staff were kept safe and to keep our media relations person informed so that she could speak with reporters when they called.

The next day started out as a mild, cloudy day with weather predictions of heavy snow for the late afternoon. By 7:00 a.m., I was in my SPCA vehicle, followed by five more vehicles in a convoy headed down the highway to meet with officer Rosie Tandry by 9:00 a.m.

I was also pleased that Dave from the wildlife facility had offered to come along and bring his tranquilizer gun as well. He would be able to take two of the wolves at his facility, so he also brought his truck and several large animal crates.

When we arrived at Ms. Swinger's wolf sanctuary, Rosie had everything organized, as I had come to expect from her.

Senior Inspector Granby would remain at the end of the laneway to block media and gawkers from entering the property. Two MNR conservation officers were there to document where all of the animals were going, as well as to oversee the humane euthanasia of the four wolf/dog hybrids. A local veterinarian that had some experience dealing with captive wildlife was present and could stay all day if needed. A local horse farmer had arrived with a two-horse trailer to take the pony. The police had attended initially, but as we had no plans to enter the house and Swinger was not on the property, the officer had left to attend other duties.

Tandry even had a friend of hers come with his snowplow to make sure we had a large enough area cleared that would accommodate all of our trucks.

Since Rosie's initial visit to the wolf sanctuary, the temperature had been slowly rising as spring was approaching, and even though we were expecting a significant snowstorm that afternoon, it was above freezing in the morning. The thaw had created large pools of melted snow, revealing a winter's worth of feces and urine as well as the liquid effluent from the guts of the dead animals that had been fed to the wolves.

The putrid smell was enough to make us all gag, but we were grateful for a fairly stiff breeze—the breeze that would eventually plunge the temperature below freezing and bring heavy snow with it.

Dave and I set up our respective tranquilizer guns and equipment on the tailgate of one of the pickup trucks, and the vet prescribed the drugs for the first couple of darts for the first pen containing two adult wolves. Other SPCA staff members were busy catching and loading the pony and catching the raccoons from their cage, as well as the two foxes.

Dave and I, now armed with our tranquillizer guns, set up on opposite sides of the first pen of wolves, taking care to ensure that we were not in each other's line of sight. The wolves were very active and trotting back and forth, in and out of their den, around exposed rib cages of cattle corpses, making it impossible to get a good shot.

I would never put one of my staff in a dangerous situation or ask them to do something that would risk their safety, so when it became apparent that the only way we were going to get a good shot at the fleshy part of the rear end of the wolves was to enter their pen, I said that I would do it.

Fortunately, the animals were more afraid of me than I was of them. They simply increased their pace in order to keep distance between them and me as I maneuvered around the pen. Sloshing through the liquid effluent, I was grateful that my rubber boots didn't leak. After the first wolf ran past me, splashing the brown liquid into my face, I was sure to close my eyes and mouth for future passes.

I delivered the first dart, and it hit a large black wolf with a sharp *thwack* in his right thigh and stayed there. The second dart followed shortly thereafter into the second animal. I left the pen to let the animals settle down and for the drug to take effect.

Dave and the vet had set up a good system of loading darts and keeping track of drug doses, times darts made impact and evidence of drowsy wolves.

In many situations involving the capture of wildlife that I have been involved with, it has been my experience that the veterinarian prescribing the drugs usually leans to the lower doses to be safe. This often results in the need for a second, or "top-up" dart being fired into the same animal in order to get a safe level of sedation. However, in this case, the wolves were dropping pretty quickly and were completely asleep.

As we began taking the sleeping animals out of their pen and placing them in a recumbent position (laying upright on their chest to prevent aspiration) in their straw-bedded crates, the vet gave each animal a quick exam and, as we had previously decided, vaccinated each of them.

There is a very distinct and unpleasant sound when an intramuscular injection hits bone. After the vet had unleashed a string of colourful expletives, he told us that the wolves were grossly underweight. This fact had gone unnoticed by us, since the wolves all had a thick winter coat and appeared active, and we had not had our hands on any of them until now.

Officer Tandry, standing right behind the vet, was quick to ask his opinion of the type and quantity of feed given to the wolves and if he would agree that they had been neglected. With an affirmative reply from the vet, Tandry turned to me and said, "I'm going to charge her. I don't care how noble her cause was or how cooperative she has been, this is criminal neglect." I definitely agreed with Tandry but urged her to put those thoughts aside and focus on the job at hand, as it was now early afternoon and the snow had started to fall.

As wolves were beginning to recover from their drug-induced naps in secure cages in the back of various SPCA trucks, the vet cleared each of them and the drivers headed out for their assigned destination. Each vehicle had at least two wolves in it, and several zoos were awaiting their arrival.

The last vehicle containing animals to leave was a full-sized van with four wolves and two drivers. Senior Inspector Granby and Officer Boudouin were my only two officers who spoke enough French to be the lucky drivers to take the animals to the zoo in Quebec. As luck would have it for them, although they had the longest journey, they were heading in the same eastern direction as the approaching storm and managed to stay just ahead of the nasty weather all the way to central Quebec.

The others were not so lucky. By the time they were all on their way across central Ontario, they were all driving in blinding snow.

Throughout this operation, I had called the acting CEO a couple of times to keep him informed of our progress. Senior Inspector Grandy had done several media interviews at the end of the laneway and had called the provincial office to keep our media person informed of our progress as well.

I had instructed each officer to call my cell phone when they were safe at home, no matter what time it was. I received the last call just after 3:00 a.m. and was pleased that all of the animals had arrived alive and well at each of their destinations and all of my staff were also home safe.

The following day at the provincial office, the acting CEO was laughing when he recounted our telephone conversations to other senior staff members. "The Chief sounded like he was all hyped up, talking a mile a minute." Then turning to me, "You sure do love your job."

There was some gratification when Ms. Lillian Swinger was found guilty in court of neglecting her wolves. She had since lost ownership of the property to the bank and had applied for welfare. The judge realized that a fine was pointless in this case, and there was no justification for putting her in jail. Her penalty was that she had to surrender the rest of her animals (dogs and cats) to the SPCA and she was not allowed to own any animals for two years. The MNR also told us that she would never get a permit to keep wildlife in captivity again.

Sadly, the lion and four hybrid wolf/dogs were all put to sleep. After consulting with Dave's vet and seeking advice from several of my zoo contacts, we knew that no zoo would want to accept a blind lion, since she would likely be killed by other lions if introduced into a new group. As for the wolf/dog hybrids, it is illegal to own such an animal in this province, and the officers from the MNR were pretty insistent that they be euthanized.

The greatest reward for me came several months later in the middle of summer, when I attended one of the zoos that had adopted a pair of the wolves from us.

They had a nearby two-story observation tower where the zoo guests could climb up and look out over most of the zoo, particularly the wolf enclosure.

The enclosure was a very large, densely treed pen. One had to wait and use keen senses to observe either of the two animals in the pen. When I caught a glimpse of one of the wolves, I was very surprised to see that it had shed its winter coat, had gained lots of weight and looked very happy to be living in a clean, natural enclosure that resembled its wild habitat. Even though this was much restricted compared to the territory a wild wolf would live in, there was no evidence of the often-seen stereotypical behavior of pacing back and forth. Clearly, there was sufficient room and environmental enrichment to make the wolves feel comfortable. It sure made me feel like we had done a very good thing in getting those animals out of the so-called sanctuary.

Bull on a Rope

The first time we heard that Portuguese-style bullfighting was coming to Ontario, the chief inspector at the time, one of my predecessors, turned several shades of red and stated emphatically, "Not if I have anything to say about it!" His British military and police background shone through as he puffed his chest out and spoke with great authority.

The Chief was pretty sure that this type of activity was prohibited under the Criminal Code of Canada. I was a relatively new employee at the time, with only a half dozen years on the job, but visions of Spanish bullfights and majestic bulls being stabbed in the withers by a pompous-looking matador flashed through my head. How could we ever allow this to happen in our province!

A meeting was arranged at the provincial office of the OSPCA, which included the organizer of the proposed spectacle, the owners of the bulls that were being imported to Canada even as we met, the chief inspector of the OSPCA and just to make sure he had lots of support (and uniformed men) along for the meeting, I and three other inspectors were to attend as well.

Maud, the provincial office receptionist, had arranged for coffee, tea and some muffins to be provided. Given the nature of the meeting and the subject matter, she hoped that those items would not end up being thrown at other attendees of the meeting.

On the day in question, we all acted civilized and remained calm during the introductions, except for the fact that the Chief inspector maintained a bright red glow on his face, head and neck—high blood pressure, I expect, from restraining his desire to unleash his true feelings about bullfighting and the likelihood of it coming into our province.

Sam Flores, the organizer of the event (also the owner of the land that the event was to take place on and therefore a person who stood to make a lot of money) was very well-spoken, with a slight Portuguese accent. He assured us that Portuguese bullfighting was not at all like Spanish bullfighting. He explained that the bull would be tied on a very long rope. The rope would be secured around the bull's neck in such a way that it would not tighten or choke the animal. About six or eight men would hold the end of the very long rope, and brave young men from the audience would emerge from the safety of the viewing stands, run in front of the bull, try to touch it without getting gored then return to the safety of the sidelines. All the time, the animal is slowed in its pursuit of the brave young men by the half dozen anchormen at the other end of a rope.

After this description from Mr. Flores, during which he consulted in Portuguese frequently with his two friends, one of whom was the owner of the bulls, the Chief smiled and said, "This isn't bullfighting. This is a bull on a rope!"

This brought some smiles and a few chuckles from our newfound friends, until the Chief went on to announce that he still felt the activity constituted an offence in Canada. He would be consulting with a Crown Attorney whether the event went ahead or not.

Sam assured us the event would proceed and invited us to send as many representatives as we deemed appropriate to observe the event. The Chief said, "To gather evidence, more like!"

We all shook hands, and there were lots of smiles as the Portuguese contingent left the building. Maud was pleased to see that all of the muffins were gone and no coffee cups had been smashed.

The following day, the Chief met with the Senior Crown Attorney at the local courthouse and discussed the possibility of obtaining an injunction to stop the bull-on-a-rope event. It was decided that since the event had not taken place and there was no proof that any animals would be harmed, a court injunction would not be applied for. The Crown agreed that we should attend the event, take notes and photos, and then present the information for consideration of a charge under the criminal code.

The day of the event finally arrived. It was a warm start to what would later become a hot summer Saturday, and the fields of the Flores farm that usually had cattle at pasture on them were now full of cars, campers, tents and trailers belonging to the many spectators in attendance for the bull on a rope event.

As we walked away from our SPCA vehicles, we made sure that we kept them in sight. We didn't want anyone to vandalize them, and we might need to make a hasty retreat. We all felt like we were entering the enemy camp as hundreds of spectators noted the appearance of four men in uniforms.

We couldn't see where Sam Flores was, but we could hear his voice loud and clear over the public address system that had been set up on the farm. He spoke in English and Portuguese to the audience, which numbered in the several hundreds. Many people in the audience had obviously been drinking (a liquor permit had been obtained for the event and was clearly posted at the entrance to the farm) and responded with loud cheers to everything Sam said.

"Ladies and gentlemen! Please give a warm, Portuguese welcome to our friends from the Ontario PSAC (I suspect Joe had had a few glasses of wine as well) who are here to see our beautiful bulls and make sure that no harm comes to any of the animals." Mr. Flores sure knew how to handle a crowd. The events were soon underway.

Six large wooden crates had been set up side by side at one end of the long passageway that was created by bleachers on each side of the 100-foot-wide clearing. Each box contained a black bull, and we checked each of them to ensure that there were no cuts or scrapes on them. All of the bulls seemed in excellent physical condition.

Several men in colourful Portuguese clothing were passing a heavy rope through the back of the first crate and slipping the noose end over the head of the bull.

After Sam had whipped the audience up into a frenzy of shouts and whistles, the door of the first crate flew open. The bull-on-a-rope emerged at the trot.

From the bleachers at the side, several brave (mostly drunk) young men and, to our surprise, a couple of brave (also mostly drunk) young ladies took to the clearing between the two rows of bleachers and directly in front of the bull.

Away at a fast pace went the bull, head down, charging for the foolish people in front of him who were waving their arms and yelling at the bull. All the while, six or eight colourfully dressed, stout, older (wiser and more sober) men held onto the rope about forty feet (ten meters) behind the bull, slowing him down. Not slowing him enough for the first man in front of the bull, who was now impaled on the horns of the bull. In one swift motion, the bull sent the man flying over his shoulder to the ground. Other "brave" men caught the attention of the bull and kept it focused on moving forward away from the injured man, who was trying to get to his feet while holding his hands near his groin. A couple of other spectators quickly emerged from the stands and helped the man off the field.

Much to my surprise, I heard the Chief Inspector shout in a very loud voice, "Bulls one, men nil." Ya gotta love the British sense of humour.

After about ten minutes of bull on a rope versus inebriated Portuguese people, the bull was clearly tiring. He was released from the rope and turned loose in a separate pen. The rope was then affixed to bull number two for a repeat performance.

This continued until all of the bulls had been used and several brave (drunk) men had been taken away by ambulance.

We had taken a number of photographs and documented the day's activities in our notebooks. As we left the farm, Sam met us and thanked us for coming to the event. The Chief shook his hand, but also said he still planned to lay charges. Sam smiled and said he would expect to see him in court in the near future.

We could hear lots of music and singing as we were leaving. Clearly this was a big cultural event for many members of the Portuguese community.

Over the next couple of weeks, the Chief met with the Crown Attorney, and together they decided which section of the criminal code would be used to lay a charge against Sam Flores. A date for a trial was eventually set. On that day, the courtroom was packed, mostly with members of the Portuguese community eager to see if their bull on a rope event would be allowed to continue in the future.

After presenting the evidence we had gathered at the event and hearing testimony from the Chief Inspector, the Crown had argued that this caused undue hardship on animals and was a pointless and unnecessary activity harmful to animals. The lawyer for the defense argued that this was a cultural event steeped in centuries of tradition and so very important to the Portuguese people now living in Canada. He also pointed out that Portuguese people love and respect all animals and that the opportunity to display bravery was vital to their young men.

The judge took several hours to deliberate before handing down his verdict of not guilty. In his summation, the judge pointed out that across this country there are countless activities that could be deemed "pointless and unnecessary" by some people while being vitally important to others. He used hunting, rodeo, equestrian events, dog trials and horse racing as examples. He noted that there was no evidence that any animals had been injured or hurt. In fact, quite the opposite—people had been injured.

Portuguese-style bullfighting, or bull on a rope, continues in various parts of the province on a regular annual basis. To the best of my knowledge, no further legal action has been taken to try and stop it.

Afterword

I have mentioned that most people who get into animal welfare work, whether that is animal control, animal care or cruelty investigation work, do so because they like animals. At the same time, those people are now in a position to see people and their animals at their worst.

Some staff members are able to cope, while others simply can't take the horrors of seeing the abuse firsthand from the inside and decide to seek employment elsewhere.

For those who stick with it, everyone seems to have a coping mechanism. I'm not a psychologist, so my analysis of this subject is based on simple observation and my own coping mechanism.

I have seen good people resort to alcohol in order to cope with the things they had to deal with on the job—not a good solution. Still others, as mentioned in the book, seek professional help from a counselor or psychologist/psychiatrist, which is probably the best route to take.

When I look back on my career as a cruelty officer, I realize that I seemed to have a mechanism to become temporarily detached from the emotional aspect of the work. In other words, at the time of a major seizure, when removing animals from an abusive hoarder or other neglectful situation, no matter how horrific the state of the animals or their surroundings, I seemed to become emotionally dead at the time.

This state of detachment was indeed temporary and often when I was alone, either at home, or in my vehicle driving home, I would break down and cry—I mean sob and blubber in a very unattractive way. Usually, I could recover and enter our house appearing to just be exhausted from my recent experience.

Two odd things, though. There are some incidents that I still can't talk about (or even write about) without tearing up and having to end a conversation. I suppose those memories will remain locked inside my head until the day I die. The other odd thing is that even though I have departed from the front lines of cruelty work, I still have dreams about animals in abusive or neglectful situations. In a dream, I re-experience that odd sense of detachment and sometimes that tight gut feeling when one is faced with a very stressful situation. I often wake up with a pain in my jaw from clenching my teeth in my sleep, and my dentist has me wearing a mouth guard to prevent my teeth from wearing down because I grind them in my sleep.

I find it very upsetting to lose one of our pets. In the past couple of years, we have lost two very old dogs and one old cat, and each passing was hard for me to deal with emotionally. I try to take some solace from what my grandma said many years ago: "All dogs go to heaven."

Perhaps everyone experiences these feelings of anxiety after they retire from their job of over thirty years, but I suspect not, since most jobs don't have the same emotional aspect to them. Dealing with living beings that depend on us to relieve their suffering and provide them with the necessities of life, including affection and attention, takes an emotional toll on people.

Writing this book has been somewhat cathartic, but the mental burden of the memories of over thirty years in animal welfare is something that I will have to continue to cope with for the rest of my days.